MODERN

ART
Design, Fuse &
Quilt-As-You-Go
Sue Bleiweiss

QUILTS

stashBOOKS.

an imprint of C&T Publishing

Text copyright © 2018 by Sue Bleiweiss
Photography and artwork copyright © 2018 by C&T Publishing, Inc.

Publisher: Amy Marson

Creative Director: Gailen Runge

Acquisitions Editor: Roxane Cerda

Managing Editor: Liz Aneloski

Editor: Lynn Koolish

Technical Editor: Julie Waldman

Cover/Book Designer: April Mostek

Production Coordinator: Zinnia Heinzmann

Production Editor: Alice Mace Nakanishi

Illustrator: Valyrie Gillum

Style photography by Lucy Glover and instructional photography
by Mai Yong Vang of C&T Publishing, Inc., unless otherwise noted

Published by Stash Books, an imprint of C&T Publishing, Inc., P.O. Box 1456,
Lafayette, CA 94549

Library of Congress Cataloging-in-Publication Data
Names: Bleiweiss, Sue, author.
Title: Modern art quilts : design, fuse & quilt-as-you-go / Sue Bleiweiss.
Description: Lafayette, CA : C&T Publishing, Inc., [2018]
Identifiers: LCCN 2018010087 | ISBN 9781617456817 (soft cover)
Subjects: LCSH: Quilting. | Art quilts.
Classification: LCC TT835 .B51347 2018 | DDC 746.46--dc23
LC record available at https://lccn.loc.gov/2018010087

Printed in China

10 9 8 7 6 5 4 3 2 1

Dedication

for Olivia & Ben
be kind
be thoughtful
be true to yourself
dream big & reach for the stars

Acknowledgments

A huge thank-you to Lynn Koolish
for her superior editing skills as
well as her guidance and support
throughout the process of writing
this book. For Iris, because
Mistyfuse makes it possible
for me to create quilts the way
I want to make them. To my
friends who cheered me on
when the writing process got
overwhelming and I didn't think
I'd ever meet the deadlines—
thank you for your unwavering
support and friendship, you know
who you are and I love you all.

And, of course, to Scott, for always
encouraging me to reach for the stars
and follow my dreams.

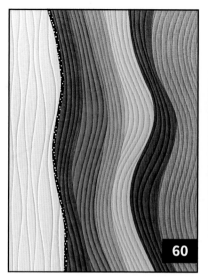

50 54 60

CONTENTS

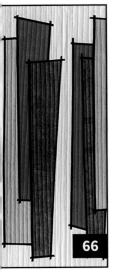

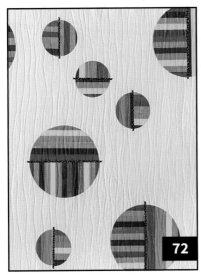

Projects

INTRODUCTION

When I made my first quilt many, many years ago I used the traditional construction method of piecing, using ¼″ seams and making sure all my corners and angles matched up. It was a torturous experience and I vowed I would never to do it again. I have great respect and admiration for quilters who have the perseverance to cut large pieces of fabric into small ones and then put them together using ¼″ seams, but it's a construction technique that I just have no patience for. That first quilting experience put me off quilting for a lot of years! So what's a quilter to do when she finds herself wanting to make modern quilts but not willing to sew a ¼″ seam? She finds another way.

And so I choose to fuse!

With no seams to sew, no shape is off limits. Circles, triangles, hexagons, curved edges, lines—whatever shape or image that I want to incorporate into my design is usable because I don't have to worry about how I will connect one shape to the other. Bias-cut edges and accuracy are not problems because when I fuse a shape in place, it stays where I put it. There are no worries about corners or intersections not lining up or which direction to press ¼″ seams. Fusing gives me an incredible amount of flexibility in my quilt designs, and that means any design that I can dream up, I can turn into a quilt.

But a successful quilt design needs more than just the flexibility of fusing to achieve a visually pleasing result and that's why I've dedicated a section of this book to a discussion about the elements of art and the principles of design. Modern quilts are typically identified by their use of high contrast, graphic designs, expansive negative space, and minimalist design. While those parameters sound easy enough to work in, a basic foundation in the principles of design will allow you to design quilts that are more likely to intrigue the viewer and elicit a *Wow!* response.

To get you started on your journey, this book features seven fused quilt projects, ranging from small to large. If you're new to fusing, I suggest you start with *Party Lights* (page 50). It's a small quilt, measuring just 13″ × 13″, with a fun design created using just squares and a few wavy lines. It's a perfect way to introduce yourself to working with fusible web without getting overwhelmed by a large project with a more complicated design.

Usually, I like to work with my own hand-dyed fabrics, but for all the projects in this book, I used solids from Cherrywood Fabrics instead. If you want to try your hand at dyeing, take a look at the method that I use (see Easy Fabric Dyeing, page 104). I prefer working with solids over prints, but I encourage you to make your quilts using the fabrics and colors that *you* like to work with. You can change the color palettes, use a combination of prints and solids, change the size of the quilts, or incorporate your own personal touches by adding imagery or shapes that you like. You can create the projects as they are or use them as a jumping off point for your own designs—the choice is yours and the possibilities are endless!

I wish you all the best in all your creative endeavors!

Sue

ART AND DESIGN

When it comes to the elements of art and design, you'll find a lot of points of view. An internet search on the subject results in more than two-million results! A search on Amazon for books on the subject returns pages and pages of titles, and each of those websites and books seems to have a different opinion and definition for what the elements of art and the principles of design are. So how do you make sense of all of it, what are the differences between elements and principles, and does it really matter?

In my opinion, it does matter, if for no other reason than this: When you have a basic understanding of the concepts to refer to, it makes it easier for you to critique your own work and evaluate what happened if your finished piece isn't quite as visually appealing as you want it to be. This is especially true when it comes to designing modern quilts because they tend to incorporate geometric or graphic elements combined with empty space. You need to know how to take a quilt that uses a single image and a limited color palette from flat and boring to a visually stunning masterpiece, and understanding the elements and principles of design helps you do just that. The following gives you an introductory outline.

Elements of Design

These are the building blocks of every piece of artwork. You can't make a piece of art without using one or more of these. Think of these as the ingredients in a recipe.

LINE

Line is where it all begins. Lines can be thick, thin, straight, wavy, horizontal, vertical, diagonal, curved, solid, or broken.

SHAPE

Shape starts as a line and once the line meets or intersects with another it becomes a shape. Shapes can be geometric or free-form. Shapes can also be formed using the negative space between objects or lines.

COLOR AND VALUE

As quilters we all know what *color* is, but color and value are probably the elements of art that are most likely to intimidate—with value, contrast, mood, complementary, triad, primary, neutrals, warm, cool, color wheels—*yikes!* Indeed, there's a lot know when it comes to the subject of color and value. My approach is…Don't overthink it! I use and combine colors, values, and hues as they speak to me and give me the visual result that I want.

You could spend weeks and months studying texts on color, but that won't leave much time for creating—work with colors and combinations that you like and don't worry about where they fall on the color wheel.

TEXTURE

Texture refers to a surface quality that can either be seen, felt, or both. Texture can be real or implied—for example, if you create an image of a cactus on your quilt by using paint, dye, fabric markers, or some other means, it can appear to be rough and sharp; but when you touch it, the surface is smooth so the texture is implied. Alternatively, if you use hand embroidery, beading, or trapunto on a quilt to create texture, they can be both seen *and* felt. You can also create texture using pleating, wrinkling, or fraying of the edge of the fabric. You can use many ways to create real texture on a quilt beyond using stitching or handwork. The use of nontraditional or mixed-media materials on the surface of a quilt can be used to create texture, such as paper, textile foils, Lutradur, rug canvas, and netting, just to name a few.

Principles of Design

These are the ways that you use the elements of art. If you think of the elements of art as the ingredients in the recipe, think of the principles of design as the way the meal is cooked and presented on the plate.

BALANCE

This refers to the distribution of the elements in the artwork. It can refer to the images, colors, textures, or space in the artwork. Balance can be symmetric (even) or asymmetric (uneven). In a symmetrical approach, the elements may be different from one another, but they're presented in such a way that the overall visual result is fairly even across the surface of the work. When the balance is asymmetric, visual harmony is created by using unrelated or an uneven number of elements, shapes, sizes, or subjects, but presenting them in such a way that the contrast or variety of the images is offset and they counterbalance each other, resulting in a visually balanced design. A butterfly is a good example of symmetrical balance. Its wings and the markings repeat on both sides of the body.

Set the Table (at right) is a good example of asymmetric balance. The variety of unrelated shapes and elements (vase, glass, apple, bottle) adds balance to the finished quilt. Imagine this quilt with just the flower vase on it—the design would look unbalanced and lopsided. The wine bottle helps create balance, not only because it fills the space to the left of the wine glass, but the height of the bottle helps provide a balance counterpoint to the flower vase. Had I put a bowl or a piece of fruit in place of the wine bottle, the entire composition would have felt off balance.

Set the Table, 39″ × 30″

MOVEMENT AND RHYTHM

These two, along with the word *motion*, are sometimes defined separately, but I see them as mostly the same. They can refer to the path your eye takes around the artwork and draws you to an area of the work the artist wants you to focus on. You can also create movement or motion by the use of repeated objects and how you arrange them. Lines can also imply movement—think of the wavy line of the water's edge along a stretch of sand.

This quilt is a great illustration of movement. The eye follows the water drops falling out of the faucet and landing in the puddle below. Movement is created with the blue droplets being forced out of the puddle from the impact of the water droplets splashing into the puddle.

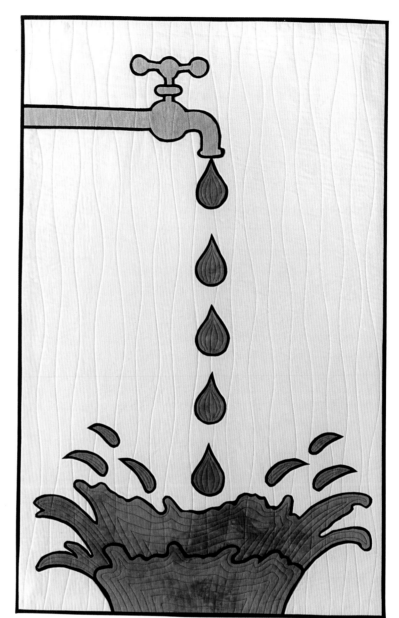

Drip, 24˝ × 38˝

CONTRAST

Contrast can refer to colors, shapes, values, sizes, textures, types of line, and so on. A lack of contrast will result in quilt that reads as flat and dull, and the visual impact of the design will be lost.

Moon Over the Concrete Jungle—original version, 55″ × 39″

Photo by Sue Bleiweiss

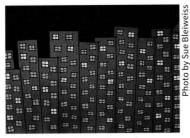

Moon Over the Concrete Jungle—second version, 55″ × 39″

Photo by Sue Bleiweiss

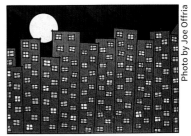

Moon Over the Concrete Jungle—final version, 55″ × 39″

Photo by Joe Offria

The designs for *Moon Over the Concrete Jungle* are an excellent lesson in contrast. In the original version, the imagery was good, but the quilt was boring and dull because of the lack of contrast. In the second version, I added some contrast to the buildings by darkening the sky. This improved the quilt quite a bit, but it still felt boring so I added the image of the moon to break up the sky, which also added just the right amount of additional contrast.

PROPORTION

Proportion refers to how the images and shapes relate and work with each other when viewed as a whole. The size of the images that are used in your quilt will affect how the viewer sees them and the overall quilt. For example, in *Set the Table* (page 11), the size of the wine glass is proportional to the size of the wine bottle it is next to, which is what you would expect the size of a wine glass in real life to be. If the wine glass was reduced in size by half, then it would be the size of the apple it's next to, and the proportion of not only the glass but the entire composition would be off.

SPACE

Space refers to the area between and around the objects—also referred to as *negative space*. Negative space can represent shapes by using the areas between objects or lines.

The Dress, 66″ × 36″

Vase with Flowers, 39″ × 30″

In *Vase with Flowers*, the negative space implies the shape of the vase.

In *The Dress*, the use of line and space comes together to form a striking image of a sophisticated elegant woman. Just eleven lines were used to create this image, placing them such a way that the image of the woman in a dress wearing a hat can be seen because the space between the lines creates shapes that are easily recognized. With the exception of the lines used to imply ruffles at the bottom the dress, none of the lines touch. It's the empty space between the lines that creates the image.

PATTERN

Pattern refers to the visual harmony or repetition that occurs when a shape, object, or element is repeated.

Stacks of Three, 46″ × 26″ (see project, page 66)

Stacks of Three illustrates the use of pattern in several ways. First is the use of the repeating shape—the elongated rectangle that is repeated in each stack across the surface. Second is the use of the same number of the shapes in each stack. Third is the use of the same color scheme in each stack. By changing the order of the colors used in each stack and the use of the bright red for contrast against the gray and the white, your eye is drawn across the quilt continuously rather than resting on a single stack.

VARIETY

Variety refers to the use of several related or unrelated elements, colors, images, shapes, and so on used to create visual interest. By varying the components in your quilt you create interest and avoid a boring result. For example, in *Stacks of Three*, if I'd used just one color instead of three for the rectangles or used the exact same layout for each stack, the lack of variety would have resulted in a very boring quilt.

EMPHASIS

Emphasis refers to the focal point of the artwork that the artist wants to highlight or draw the viewer's eye toward. In *The Dress* (previous page), I used the color red on her lips to draw your eye to her face, creating a focal point that I wanted to emphasize. A spot of color is not the only way to create emphasis though. The use of texture, shape, or size can be used to draw attention because the eye is always drawn to something that stands out as different.

UNITY

Also referred to as *harmony*, unity refers to how visually satisfying the elements and components of the artwork are; in other words, whether all the elements that are used somehow relate to one another to create a visual whole. This doesn't mean that the images used must all be the same, it means they should relate to one another in some way so that they look like they belong together. In the quilt *If I Were a Tree*, the components all relate to one another so the result is a unified image. If I had used ocean waves in place of the grass and fish in place of the leaves, neither which relate to the elements of the flowers or the tree, then the overall visual unity would be lost.

Considering that only four elements make up *If I Were a Tree* (at right)—a tree, flowers, leaves, and grass—the use of variety plays a critical role in keeping this quilt from reading as boring. The variety of sizes and shapes of the repeating image of the flowers encourages the eye to wander across the surface, looking for a place to rest. If all the flowers were the same shape and/or color, the design would be dull and monotonous.

Variety (page 15) and unity (above) all play a role in this quilt.

Design Exercises

One of the best ways to understand the concepts of art and design is to spend some time exploring and using them. Following are a few exercises to get you started. I recommend you work small, no larger than 12″ × 12″, so that you don't get overwhelmed with having to fill too much space and you can complete each piece in a reasonable amount of time.

If I Were a Tree, 40″ × 40″

Not every piece of art you make will use every element of art and principle of design, nor does it have to, but having an understanding of and being able to identify them will help you as you design, create, and critique your own quilts (see Critique, Learn, and Develop Your Personal Style, page 96).

EXERCISE 1
Color and Color Combinations

Green Leaf, 12″ × 12″

EXERCISE 2
Shape and Simplicity

Circled, 13″ × 13″

EXERCISE 3
Line and Movement

Party Lights, 13″ × 13″ (see project, page 50)

1 Create a quilt, limiting the number of colors to no more than two, but do use different values within each color. By restricting the color choices, you're free to focus on the techniques with an emphasis on composition and design. If you're stuck for ideas on what colors to choose or subjects to work with for your quilt, pull out some old magazines and cut out interesting words, phrases, and color combinations. Toss them in a paper bag and pull one out at random and use it to spark an idea. For some other ideas on how to get started, see Finding Inspiration (page 18).

Using a limited numbers of colors in a quilt can create a striking design. In this quilt, the light green fabric provides a nice contrast with the dark values of the deep green and purple fabrics. The light green draws the eye to that area, but the darker green stems keep the eye moving across the design.

2 Create a quilt using just one shape as the primary element or focal point; it could be a circle, square, triangle, or whatever shape you like.

Using a single shape as the primary element in a quilt doesn't mean that the result will be uninteresting or boring. The wavy horizontal quilting lines provide movement and encourage the eye to move across the surface where they come to rest on the circles. The odd number of brightly colored circles provides a pop of color and a focal point for the eye to rest.

3 Create a quilt that has an emphasis on using line to create movement.

Several design choices contribute to the movement of this quilt: The wavy vertical quilting lines, the undulating black lines that the blocks seem to be suspended on, and the way the blocks are offset from one another giving the impression that they're blowing in the wind. The feeling of movement would not be as obvious if I had used straight lines for the quilting and the black lines or had placed the blocks horizontally across the bottom.

FINDING INSPIRATION

Looking for Ideas

Ideas for a quilt can come from anywhere! Grab your camera and go for a walk in the woods, around the block, or around town. Be aware of what's around you as you walk—a brick walkway laid out in an interesting pattern, a row of flowers, a picket fence, a window with an intriguing pattern made by the panes, a shop window display with an interesting combination of colors or patterns. Can't get outside? Then take a look out the window. What colors and textures do you see? Do you see surfaces changed by their exposure to the elements leaving rust, decay, and layers of exposed paint?

One of my favorite places to look for ideas for quilts is at a museum. I wander around the many exhibits and just wait for something to catch my eye. It might be the details in a centuries-old vase, an Egyptian tool, or the colors and imagery in a painting by one of the old masters.

Are you a collector of teapots, figurines, stamps, vintage textiles, or something else? Perhaps one of those will provide inspiration. Or maybe you're drawn to a shape (circle, square, triangle, hexagon)—create a quilt celebrating that shape.

Sketching

One of the most important tools in my studio is my sketchbook—it's the starting point for every quilt I create. It's my visual sandbox filled with unorganized pages of simple line drawings, notes, and lists done in black pen with the occasional addition of colored pencil or watercolor paint. My sketchbooks are not meant to be an end result in themselves. They're just the beginning of my art-making process and very often provide me with a road map to realizing a creative vision brainstormed on its pages.

Pages from my sketchbooks

White base Batiks?

Various Squares of Batik

Sketches I did when I was brainstorming
ideas for *The Dress* (page 14)

Sketches for *Vase with Flowers* (page 14)

Sketches for *Set the Table* (page 11)

Using a sketchbook can go way beyond drawing images that are perfect renderings of things that you see. I'm talking about using a sketchbook as a place to make lists, brainstorm ideas, explore techniques, and yes, even do some rough sketches of what you might want your quilt to look like. There are many ways to approach using a sketchbook and there's no right way or wrong way to do it. Whatever way works for you is the right way and you'll need to experiment to find which way works best for you.

You may find that using several methods, rather than just one, works best for you. Whatever way you decide to use a sketchbook, keep a couple things in mind when choosing one:

• The first and quite possibly the most important is to make sure you choose one with paper appropriate to the technique you will be using on it. For example, if you are using wet media, such as acrylic or watercolor paint, choose a heavier-weight paper that won't tear or buckle when wet. If, however, you are using a combination of techniques in a sketchbook with lighter-weight paper and you find that you want to use wet media in it, you can glue the pages together in groups of two or three to give them the body they need to hold up to the paint that you're using. Another option is to work separately on heavier paper and then glue that to a page in your book. You could also keep pages in a box or folder, but gluing them into your sketchbook ensures that they won't get lost or tossed away accidentally.

• Another thing to keep in mind when choosing a sketchbook is the binding. This is really a matter of personal taste—you may find that a spiral-bound book that lies flat when opened is more suitable to your style of working than a hardcover one that doesn't. I prefer using a 5″ × 8″ one that lies flat when open. The pages are just large enough to provide enough space to work within without being so large that the plain pages become over-whelming. I don't use wet media in my sketchbooks and prefer to work with colored pencil or markers when I want to add color to my sketches, so I can choose a sketchbook with a lighter-weight paper.

Collage

I get a lot of catalogs and magazines in the mail, but rather than just tossing them into the recycle bin, I set them aside and save them for days in the studio when I'm not feeling particularly inspired. On those days, I grab my scissors and glue stick and look through the pile, cutting out whatever appeals to me. It might be a color, shape, a phrase or word, combination of colors, or a texture. I'll sort all the clippings and then glue them onto sketchbook pages using a permanent glue stick, so that I can flip through them later for inspiration.

Pages from my collage sketchbook

ART IN FIBER

Notan

Notan is a Japanese word meaning dark-light, and when applied to matters of design can be expanded to reference positive and negative and the balance between the two. Exploring the principles of *notan* can be a helpful exercise to do when searching for ideas for a modern quilt. In fact, *Inside Out* (page 78) was inspired by this technique. For a more comprehensive study of *notan*, pick up a copy of the book *Notan: The Dark-Light Principle of Design* by Dorr Bothwell and Marlys Mayfield.

MATERIALS

• Black construction paper

• White paper, at least 11″ × 14″

• Glue stick

• Scissors or craft knife

• Light-colored pencil (white, yellow, or silver) can also be helpful.

EXPANDED SQUARES

I remember doing this fun exercise in my high school art class. Start with simple shapes, and as you get comfortable with the technique, you can branch off into more complex ones. The object is to cut shapes from a square and glue them down on a piece of paper, mirroring the space they were cut from. The only rule to this exercise is that every shape you cut must be glued to the white paper. You can't throw anything anyway; otherwise, the integrity of the square is compromised.

1. Cut a piece of black construction paper 6″ × 6″. Draw a 6″ × 6″ square in the center of a piece of white paper. *Fig. A*

2. Draw 2 simple shapes on the black square. Cut these shapes out and glue them in place on the white paper, using the square you drew as a guideline. The shapes should be placed as the mirror image from the space they were cut from. *Figs. B & C*

A. 6″ × 6″ black square and 6″ × 6″ drawn square on white paper

B. The 2 simple shapes drawn on the square

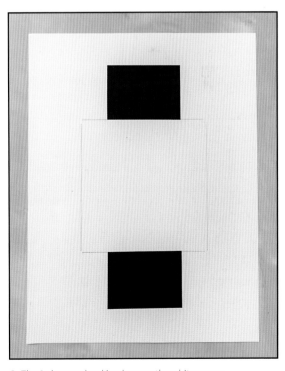

C. The 2 shapes glued in place on the white paper

Finding Inspiration

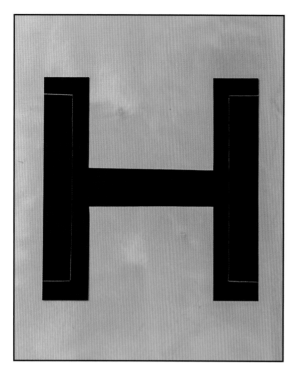

D. Draw 2 more shapes on the remains of the black square.

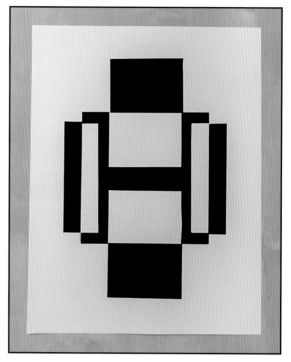

E. Glue the rest of the shapes on the white paper.

3. Draw 2 more shapes on what remains of the original black square, cut them out, and glue them along with what's left of the original black square in place on the white paper. *Figs. D & E*

Now that you've got the basic directions of how to expand the square, you can branch off and create more complex designs. *Figs. F–I*

F. This example incorporates the addition of a circular shape and a shape within a shape.

G. The addition of a curved edge creates movement.

H. A wavy edge encourages the eye to dance around the square.

I. You don't have to limit yourself to geometric shapes.

DECONSTRUCTED SHAPES

In this exercise, you take a shape apart and then put it back together again, creating an abstraction of the shape you started with. Start with a 5″ × 5″ square cut from black construction paper. Cut it apart in random shapes and then glue the pieces to a piece of white paper, leaving space between the pieces. The space you leave between the pieces becomes an integral part of the composition.

 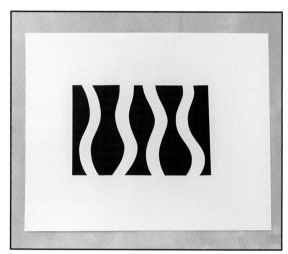

Deconstructed 5″ × 5″ squares

TIP // Create Fusible Paper

If you don't have a glue stick, before you cut your black paper into 5″ × 5″ squares, put a layer of fusible web on the back. When you cut the black square into pieces, just place them on the white paper, cover with a pressing sheet, and press with a hot iron to fuse the pieces in place.

You can expand on this exercise by using different shapes, such as circles and leaves. Any of these designs can be easily replicated using fabric as they are or used as a jumping off point for further study.

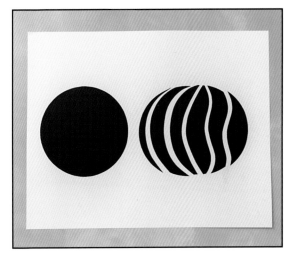

Deconstructed circles

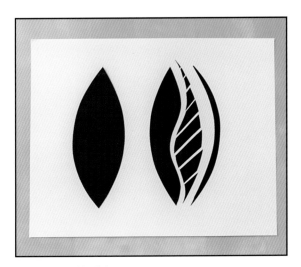

Deconstructed leaf shapes

TOOLS AND MATERIALS

All quilters have their own preferences when it comes to the tools, materials and brands that they like to use, and I'm no exception to that rule.

I encourage you to experiment with different brands and sizes to find the ones that you like best. Whatever tools you use in your studio, be sure to keep them clean and in good working order, and always use the right tool for the right job. There's nothing more frustrating than trying to cut fabric with a dull rotary cutter or sewing with the wrong-size needle in your sewing machine.

Quilting tools and materials

Tools and Materials

Fusing Tools and Supplies

FUSIBLE WEB

Fusible web is one of the most important (if not *the* most important) tools in my studio. It's the primary construction technique that I use to create all my quilts, whether they are meant to hang on the wall or be draped over the sofa. The only fusible product I use in my studio is Mistyfuse (by Attached Inc.). It's lightweight and solvent-free, it doesn't add any bulk or stiffness to my quilts, and it creates a strong reliable bond. These qualities are essential to my construction process because my quilts are created in layers, which means by the time I am ready to quilt the final layers, I can end up having to stitch through up to six, seven, or more layers of fused fabrics. Using Mistyfuse ensures that I won't have any trouble stitching through all those layers, and I don't have to deal with any of those little beads of glue that build up on the needle when using other brands (see Fusing Basics, page 38).

PRESSING SHEETS

If you're working with a brand of fusible web that does not come backed with a nonstick paper you can use either Silicone Release Paper (by C&T Publishing), Reynolds parchment paper (in rolls or precut sheets), or a Teflon pressing sheet as your press cloth.

IRONS

You can't work with fusible web without an iron. I use a dry iron in my studio, which is an iron that has no steam holes in the soleplate, and I always have my iron turned up to the highest heat setting because I only work with cotton fabric.

Basic fusing supplies

Cutting Tools

You can find a number of tools and ways to cut fabric into the shapes you want.

ROTARY CUTTERS

Many different types of rotary cutters are available to today's quilters, so experiment to find the one that feels good in your hand and that you like best. I have several different sizes that I like to use depending on the thickness of the fabric and the shape I'm cutting. The 60 mm and 45 mm are great for long general cuts with a ruler; the 28 mm and 18 mm are easier to control for precision, template, or freehand cuts.

TIP // Safety First
I know you probably know this, but I'd be remiss if I didn't add this warning: *Rotary cutting blades are essentially round single edge razor blades and are sharp enough that they can create a deep, damaging cut requiring stitches or worse.* Never, ever take your eyes off the cutter when you are making a cut and always be aware of where your free hand is in relation to where you are making your cut. The hand that is holding the ruler in place should be lying flat on the ruler and no part of your hand or fingers should be near the cutting edge.

ACRYLIC RULERS

Acrylic rulers come in a wide variety of lengths, widths, and shapes. To prevent the ruler from slipping while cutting, use a nonslip ruler or put small nonslip dots on the underside of the ruler that grab hold of the fabric.

TIP // DIY Nonstick Dots
Make your own nonslip dots with some fine sandpaper and double-stick tape: Put a layer of double-stick tape on the back side of a piece of fine sandpaper, cut small squares or use a hole punch to cut circles, and then stick the cut-out sandpaper to the underside of your acrylic ruler.

SCISSORS

When it's not practical to use a rotary cutter, I use scissors. I keep a range of different sizes on hand. Whatever brand you use, make sure you keep them clean and sharp so you don't have to struggle to make smooth, even cuts.

DIE CUTTERS

If you're faced with cutting large quantities of the same shape, consider using a die cutter. I have two Sizzix cutters in my studio: a Big Shot that cuts 6″-wide dies and a Big Shot Pro that can cut dies up to 12″ wide. These machines can cut much more than geometric shapes; you can choose from hundreds of dies, ranging from letters and numbers to shapes in a variety of themes. These handy machines operate on a hand crank system, are easy to use, and make clean, accurate, consistent cuts through several layers of fabric at once.

TIP // Always Fuse First
Put a layer of fusible web on the back side of your fabric *before* using it in your die cutting machine. This will ensure that the fusible goes all the way to the edge of the cut shape for better adhesion when fused to your project.

The Middle Layer

Because my quilts are created to hang on the wall, I use wool felt instead of traditional quilt batting as my middle layer. I prefer to use the 65/35 rayon/wool felt from National Nonwovens because it adds body without adding any loft, and I like the way my quilts hang as a result. I don't recommend using it in a quilt that is going to be washed though, because it will shrink and pucker quite a bit. To remove creases and any other wrinkles from the felt, I lay it flat on my ironing surface, spritz it with water, and then iron it with a hot iron. You can usually find the 65/35 or the 80/20 version in 36″- or 72″-wide bolts at most larger fabric supply stores, or ask your local quilt shop to stock it for you.

If you are making a quilt to *use* rather than display, you have a lot of batting options to choose from. You'll find synthetic, wool, cotton, bamboo, silk, and blends of different types just to name a few, and each type has its own pros and cons.

The 100% cotton battings are warm with a nice drape, but they will shrink anywhere from 3% to 5%. Wool and silk battings can be costly, but they are lightweight and have a nice soft drape. Synthetic polyester battings are inexpensive, but they tend to be a bit stiffer and don't drape well. They also have a tendency to "beard" (see What Is Bearding?), and because they're polyester, they don't take heat well, so they're not a good choice for fusible projects.

In addition, you can choose a batting made from a blend of different fibers. Using a blend typically gives you a combination of the pros and cons of each fiber, and they are usually less expensive than using a 100% natural fiber batting.

What Is Bearding?

Bearding is a term used to describe when the batting works its way up through the surface of the quilt to the outside. Your best defense from bearding is to avoid using loosely woven fabric. The tighter the weave, the harder it will be for the batting fibers to work their way through it.

Sewing Machines

All the quilts and projects in this book were made and quilted on my BERNINA 740 sewing machine, which can sew a variety of different stitches as well as be used for free-motion quilting. Whatever sewing machine you have in your studio, make sure you keep it free of lint and dust. I always give my machine a good cleaning after each project and sometimes halfway through a large project if I see that I'm generating a lot of lint. I use only Schmetz brand sewing needles in my machine because they're readily available and I can rely on the quality. I keep a supply of 80/20 and 90/40 universal needles on hand, and I change the needle frequently to avoid threading and stitching problems.

I don't do much free-motion quilting, but when I do, I find it easier if I am wearing a pair of nonslip gloves. I like to clip the tops of the fingers off of the gloves so that I can perform nimble tasks, such as changing the bobbin or machine thread, without having to take them off.

Thread

I admit to being a bit persnickety about the thread that I use in my studio, and I always recommend buying the best quality threads that you can. Avoid the cheap bargain-bin ten-spools-for-a-dollar threads because they are not really the bargain they appear to be. They are typically made from inferior materials and will break and shred when used, and you may also see color variations within a spool as you sew.

I prefer to sew with 100% cotton thread in either 40-weight or 50-weight, and I generally work with threads from Superior Threads, Aurifil, and Gütermann. I keep a wide range of colors and types on hand in my studio so that no matter what color fabric I'm ready to start quilting on, I have a coordinating thread for it. The exception to my 100% cotton rule is when it comes to the bobbin. I use Superior Threads' MonoPoly thread in my bobbins for a few reasons: I can get a ton of it on the bobbin at once which means fewer stops to change and refill the bobbin; it's a clear thread, so I don't have to worry about it not matching the top thread color; and because I quilt the layers of my quilt as I go, the backs look neater than they would if I use many different colors in the bobbin.

Marking Tools

PENS AND PENCILS

Marking a quilt top to create lines to guide your quilting stitches can be done in a number of ways. My favorite way is to use iron-off chalk. I fill a standard rolling chalk marker with iron-off chalk and mark my quilting lines. Whatever chalk doesn't brush off during the quilting process is easily ironed away. Other options include pens and pencils that have ink that washes out or fades away after a period of time or pencils that produce a line that can be erased from the surface of the fabric using a special eraser. You should always test any marking tool on scrap piece of your fabric before using it on your final project to make sure it will perform the way you anticipate.

CHALK PAPER

Transdoodle (by Attached Inc.) is a nonwax chalk-based transfer paper that I use a lot in my studio. It is an 8½″ × 11″ chalk-coated paper and easily brushes off the surface of the fabric it's used on. The sheets come in white, yellow, and blue and can be used over and over again until no chalk remains; because it is not wax-based, you can iron over the surface without fear of it permanently fixing to the fabric or your iron.

Some choices of marking tools

ESSENTIAL TECHNIQUES

Fusing Basics

All the projects in this book use fusing as the primary construction technique. You can find many fusible products on the market, and you should experiment with them to find the one that works the best for you. I prefer to work with Mistyfuse fusible web because it's lightweight and doesn't add any bulk or stiffness to my quilts, which is critical when I'm creating a design composed of many layers that I will have to quilt through.

I like to prefuse all my fabric so that when I'm ready to start creating, I can just pull pieces off the shelf and it's ready to cut and use. I fuse a layer of Mistyfuse to one side of the fabric, let it cool completely, and then fold it up and put it away.

TIP // Always make sure the fusible is completely cool before you fold the fabric (or use it in a die-cutting machine) or else the residual heat may cause the fabric to stick together.

1. Place the fabric that you want to add the fusible to on your ironing surface wrong side up.

2. Place a layer of fusible web on top of the fabric and then cover with a pressing sheet (page 34), and press with a hot iron. There is no need to use steam. Some fusible web, such as Mistyfuse, can take a lot of heat so you don't have to worry about overheating it. Be sure to check the manufacturer's instructions if you use a different fusible product.

3. Make sure you iron the entire area well and let it cool for a few moments before you pull the pressing sheet off the surface. If you remove it while the surface is still very hot, you may end up pulling the fusible off with it.

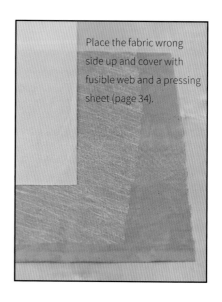

Place the fabric wrong side up and cover with fusible web and a pressing sheet (page 34).

CLEANING YOUR IRON

It's important to keep your iron's soleplate clean, otherwise you may transfer some fusible residue to your fabric that will leave marks and stains that can't be removed. At some point you will end up getting fusible web on the soleplate of your iron. It's inevitable and it happens to everyone who uses fusible—so when it happens, don't panic!

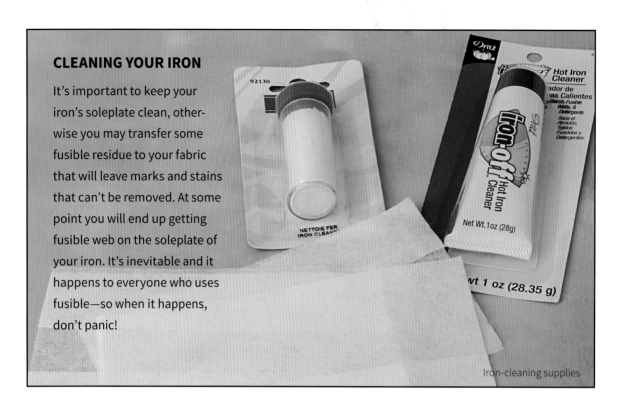

Iron-cleaning supplies

Following are three of my favorite products for cleaning my iron:

Fabric softener sheet   I keep a stack of unused, unscented dryer fabric softener sheets in my studio. When I accidentally iron over the fusible, I put a dryer fabric softener sheet on a scrap piece of fabric and run the hot iron over it. The dryer fabric softener sheet may smoke a little bit, but it will take the fusible right off the soleplate. Always iron on a scrap piece of fabric after doing this as there may be some residual oils from the dryer sheet left on the iron soleplate.

Bohin Iron Cleaner   This cleaner looks like a stick of chalk and it does a great job of cleaning a messy iron soleplate that has older stuck-on gunk. Rub the stick over the hot iron soleplate and then iron on a piece of scrap cloth. The stick will melt once it touches the hot iron so make sure you're working over a scrap piece of cloth when you do this.

Dritz Iron-Off Hot Iron Cleaner   This paste-like cleaner also works on a hot iron and is the one I turn to when the iron soleplate looks so bad that it seems the only option is to throw it away and replace it. This cleaner will cause a bit of smoke, so it's best to use in front of an open window or outside. It does a great job of removing iron gunk that the first two cleaning options don't.

TIP // If you are using Silicone Release Paper or parchment paper as your pressing sheet, clip a small amount off the lower right-hand corner. When you reuse the sheet, make sure the clipped edge is always on the lower right, which will protect your iron from picking up any residual fusible that's left on the paper.

CREATING FABRIC LETTERS

If you want to add words to your quilt, there's an easy way to do it without having to reverse any of your letters first. This technique works with any shape but it's particularly helpful when working with text and numbers.

A.

1. Trace or write your letters onto a piece of Silicone Release Paper or parchment paper, using a No. 2 pencil. *Fig. A*

2. Place your prefused fabric on top, with the fusible side against the pencil tracing. *Fig. B*

B.

3. Press with a hot iron and then peel off the Silicone Release Paper or parchment paper. The pencil mark will have transferred to the fabric. *Figs. C & D*

4. Cut out the letters along the pencil line and they're ready to fuse to your project. *Fig. E*

C.

D.

TIP // If you're using a dark-colored fabric, such as black or deep navy, use a light-colored pencil, such as white or yellow instead of a No. 2 pencil.

E.

Quilt-As-You-Go

For a lot of quilters, especially beginners, deciding how to quilt a project can be the most challenging and stressful part of the quilt making process. When I first started making quilts, I almost dreaded finishing the quilt top because it would mean having to decide how to quilt it. I never could get the hang of how to incorporate those beautiful free-motion motifs, such as feathers, florals and scrolls, into my overall design without letting them become the focal point of the quilt. When I create a quilt I want the first thing my viewer to notice is the imagery and the colors, *not* the quilting stitches—in my quilts, the quilting is meant to be a supporting player.

I use a unique quilt-as-you-go method, quilting each layer as it's completed rather than waiting until I'm finished with the entire quilt and then adding all the quilting. For example, in *Connect the Boxes* (next page), I quilted the white background completely before I fused the large colored boxes on top. I quilted the large colored boxes before I added the smaller boxes on top. You might be wondering why I would bother to quilt an area that I'm going to cover up anyway. I do this for a few reasons.

- It's a lot faster to quilt the entire top without having to quilt around shapes or to start and stop creating a lot of thread tails that you have to deal with later.

- I like that when you get up close to the quilting, the stitching lines are unbroken because the quilting lines are continuous.

- The allover quilting adds an additional layer of stability to the overall finished quilt.

TIP // Make It Opaque

Sometimes when I layer one fabric on top of another, the quilting and the color of the fabric beneath may show through. This is especially true when I'm fusing a light color on top of a dark one. To counteract this effect, fuse the lighter fabric to a piece of white fabric to make it more opaque.

TIP // False Backs

I like to cover the back of each of my quilts that will be displayed on the wall with a false back before I trim the quilt to size and put the binding on. I fuse a brightly colored print to the back of the quilt and then I trim the quilt to size. This false back serves two purposes: It covers up all the messy stitching, and it adds an additional layer of stability to the quilt, which helps it hang nice and straight. The only caveat to putting on a false back is that if you're thinking about submitting your quilt to a juried show, make sure they are okay with having the stitching on the back side covered.

Connect the Boxes, 40″ × 40″

Note: All the quilts in this book were quilted with the feed dogs up and the walking foot engaged. Most often I use straight lines that follow the shape of the image that I'm quilting or gentle curving wavy lines.

Binding

Every quilter has a favorite binding technique. Mine is a bit unconventional in that I bind each edge separately, don't miter my corners, and I use fusible web in place of pins.

FOUR-STEP BINDING

1. You'll need 4 strips (one for each edge of the quilt) 2″ wide by the length of the quilt edge plus 3″. If your strips are not long enough or you want to create a multicolor binding, sew shorter strips together to create a longer strip.

2. Sew 2 of the binding strips along opposite edges (left and right *or* top and bottom) of the quilt, right sides together, using a ¼″ seam allowance.

3. Press the binding strips to the outer edge of the quilt and then turn the quilt over so the back side is facing up. Press the binding strips in half lengthwise to set the crease. Trim any excess binding along the top and bottom to be flush with the edge of the quilt. *Fig. A*

4. Cut strips of fusible web 1″ wide and fuse them along the length of the folded/pressed binding strip. Turn the binding to the back of the quilt and press it to fuse it in place. *Fig. B*

Repeat Steps 2 and 3 with the other edges of the quilt, but leave a 1″ tail of binding extended past the edges of the quilt. Fold the tail ends over the edge of the quilt toward the back and press. Cut strips of fusible web 1″ wide and fuse them along the length of the folded/pressed binding strip. Turn the binding strip to the back of the quilt as you did in Step 4 and press it to fuse it in place. *Figs. C–E*

Even though the binding is fused in place, it's a good idea to hand stitch the binding to make sure that it won't pull away during washing, rolling, or traveling, if your quilt is going to be exhibited. Because the binding is fused in place, there's no need to use pins, which makes the hand stitching go much faster and pain-free, with no risk of poking yourself with a pin.

TIP // Don't Rush

Make sure you apply enough heat for long enough to fuse the binding strips in place. If you rush through this step, you may not get enough heat through the layers of fabric to adequately activate the fusible.

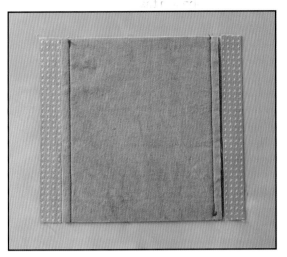

A. Press the binding strips in half lengthwise to set the crease.

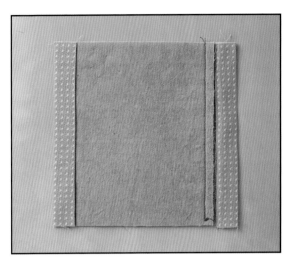

B. Turn the binding strips to the back and fuse in place.

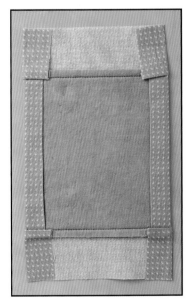

C. Fold excess 1″ in and press.

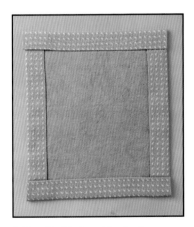

D. Fuse the binding strips in place.

E. Binding viewed from the front

Labels

Regardless whether your quilt is going to hang on a wall, be tossed on a sofa, or used on a bed, you should put a label on it. I print my labels on 100% cotton Inkjet Fabric Sheets (by Jacquard) and I include the following information:

Quilt name

Year completed

Techniques used

Artist statement specific to the quilt
(see Artist Statement, page 100)

My name and website

Work in Progress
2017
hand dyed fabric, machine quilted
Created for the D@8 2017 exhibit "personal iconography"

When it comes to personal iconography and I think of the elements and symbols that are associated with my work, it's a short list:

black outlines
bright colors
hand dyed
whimsical imagery

and while this quilt is a reflection of those four elements, it's also a reflection of where I am on my artistic journey. That is to say that I, as well as my art, are always a work in progress.

Sue Bleiweiss
sue@suebleiweiss.com

If you are planning on washing your quilt, make sure that the fabric sheets and the printer ink you are using are washable and won't run when wet. For quilts that are going to travel to be exhibited, I add an additional label with my address, phone number, and email address. I've had the experience of my quilt getting separated from its box during shipping across the country, but because I had put a label on the back with my name and address, they were able to identify the quilt and return it to me—so learn from my experience.

Hanging Sleeve

Among the many ways you can make a hanging sleeve for a quilt, the following is my favorite. It's a little more work than a standard folded sleeve, but I prefer it because the sleeve has a gusset that makes the quilt hang nicer when hung on a pole or tube as opposed to a flat rod.

1. Cut a piece of fabric 9″ wide by 2″ shorter than the width of your quilt. With the fabric wrong side up, fold in the short (9″) edges to the wrong side ½″ and press. Fold the edges in again ½″ to encase the raw edge and press well. Machine stitch them to secure them in place and then press. *Fig. A*

2. Fold the sleeve lengthwise, wrong sides together, and press the fold really well.

This fold line will be used as a guide in the next step, so make sure you press it really well to set it in place. *Fig. B*

3. Open the sleeve. With the wrong side up, fold each long edge to the pressed fold line (wrong sides together) and press them well. These fold lines will be very important in the next step, so make sure you press them really well to set them. *Fig. C*

Modern Art Quilts

With right sides together, sew the sleeve along the long edge, using a ½″ seam allowance. Turn the sleeve right side out and repress those fold lines from Step 3 to make sure they're set really well. *Fig. D*

4. Place the sleeve on the top back side of the quilt 1″–2″ down from the top, with the seamed side of the sleeve against the quilt and centered between the 2 outer edges. Hand sew the sleeve to the quilt along the 2 fold lines, keeping your stitches close to the edge of the sleeve. I also like to stitch long the 2 short edges as well—this ensures that the rod used to hang the quilt will be fed through the sleeve and not in the space between it and the back of the quilt. *Fig. E*

TIP // If you use fuse the sleeve in place on the back of your quilt, you can avoid using pins to secure it in place while you hand stitch it to the back of the quilt.

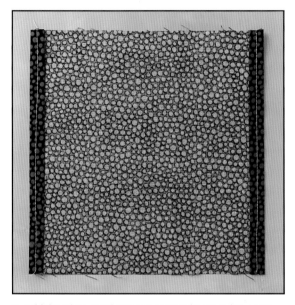

A. Fold the edges in ½″ twice to encase the raw edge, press and machine stitch. *Note:* I used white thread in this example so you can see my stitching lines, but ordinarily I would use a thread color that matches the fabric.

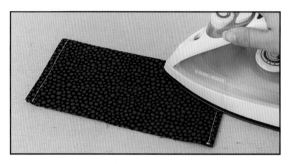

B. Fold the sleeve in half lengthwise and press well.

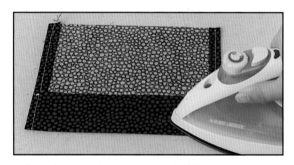

C. Press the long edges to the center fold line.

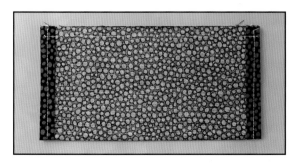

D. Press the long edges to the center fold line.

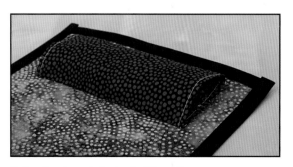

E. Sew the sleeve to the back of the quilt.

Essential Techniques

PUTTING IT ALL TOGETHER

Now that you have a foundation of the elements and principles from Art and Design (page 8), it's time to combine them with the methods in Essential Techniques (page 38) and make some quilts!

Remember that all the quilts in this book can be made as they are or you can use them as a jumping off point for your own unique designs. To help you think about ways to do that, I've included a Make It Your Own sidebar for each project—break out your sketchbook and colored pencils and sketch some new designs that combine some of the elements from these projects with your own ideas, using what you've learned from Principles of Design (page 11). Start with a small change and see where it leads you.

I've also included an Art and Design Critique sidebar for each project. These critiques highlight how the principles of design play a role in the success of the visual impact of each quilt. Keep these critiques in mind when you are altering and customizing them to create your own unique designs. They'll help you understand why I made the choices I did when I designed the original projects and help you make your own decisions.

Whatever you decide to do, whether it's making the projects as they are or customizing them to your own style of working, remember to enjoy the creative process and have fun with it!

Party Lights

Finished quilt: 13″ × 13″

Party Lights was inspired by the row of twinkling lights that hang over my outdoor dining area. It's a perfect project to start with if you're new to fusing. Make it using the colors I have or add your own personal touch by swapping a small scale black-and-white print for the solid black, changing the gray background to white, or using prints or batiks for the lights.

Materials

FABRICS

Gray: 15″ × 15″

Black: 18″ × 22″

Lime green: 4″ × 4″

Teal: 4″ × 4″

Purple: 4″ × 4″

Orange: 4″ × 4″

Magenta: 4″ × 4″

Wool felt: 15″ × 15″
(see The Middle Layer, page 36)

Backing for false back (optional):
14″ × 14″ (see Tip: False Backs, page 42)

OTHER SUPPLIES AND TOOLS

Fusible web: 1 package 2½ yards × 20″
(I prefer Mistyfuse.)

Muslin (optional): 15″ × 15″
(see Construct the Base, page 52)

Pressing sheet: Your choice
(see Pressing Sheets, page 34)

Cutting

Black: 4 strips 2½″ × 18″
(Set these aside to use for the binding.)

Important: *Before cutting the following pieces, fuse a layer of fusible web to the wrong side of each piece of fabric (see Fusing Basics, page 38).*

Lime green: 2″ × 2″   **Orange:** 2″ × 2″

Teal: 2″ × 2″   **Magenta:** 2″ × 2″

Purple: 2″ × 2″

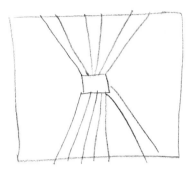

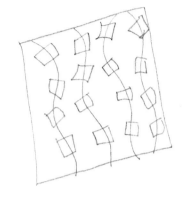

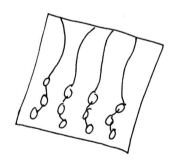

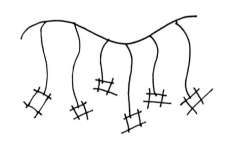

Sketches for *Party Lights*

CONSTRUCT THE BASE

Note: Putting a layer of muslin on the back side of the wool felt is optional, but I never skip this step; for quilts that will be hung on the wall, the muslin adds a bit of body and helps the quilt hang flat and straight.

1. Fuse the muslin to one side of the wool felt.

2. Fuse the gray fabric to the other side of the wool felt.

3. Quilt the gray background using wavy vertical lines randomly spaced ½″–¾″ apart across the surface (see Quilt-As-You-Go, page 42).

4. Trim the quilt to 13″ × 13″.

ADD THE LIGHTS

1. Place the quilt top on your pressing surface with the wavy quilting lines running vertically. Put the 5 colored 2″ × 2″ squares along the bottom edge of the quilt. Space them randomly and tilt them in one direction or the other. Iron to fuse the squares in place. *Fig. A*

2. Quilt the 5 squares using randomly spaced quilting lines.

3. Fuse a layer of fusible web to the wrong side of the remaining black fabric and, using a rotary cutter, freehand cut 5 wavy strips, varying the width as you cut. *Fig. B*

   Place these 5 strips on the quilt, running from the top of the quilt edge to the colored squares. Iron to fuse them in place. *Fig. C*

4. Using a rotary cutter and ruler, cut 5 strips ranging from ⅛″ to ¼″ wide from the black fabric along the long edge.

5. Fuse the strips along the raw edge of each of the colored squares, letting the black strips extend a little beyond the edge of each shape. *Fig. D*

6. With black thread in the top of the sewing machine, stitch down the center of all the black lines.

FINISH THE QUILT

1. Fuse the false back fabric to the back side of the quilt and trim off any excess.

2. Bind the quilt using the 4 dark gray 2″ × 45″ strips and either my method Four-Step Binding (page 44) or your favorite binding technique.

3. Add a label and a hanging sleeve (page 46) to the back of the quilt.

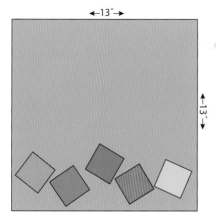

A. Fuse the lights in place.

B. Vary the width as you cut.

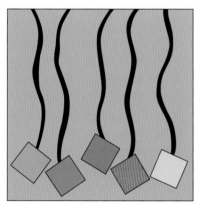

C. Fuse the strips in place.

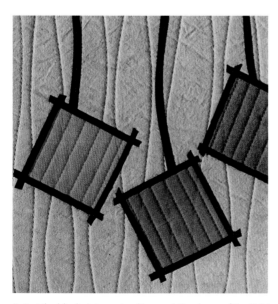

D. Let the black strips extend beyond the shape of the light.

Make It Your Own

• Change the shape of the lights. It may seem like a subtle change that won't make much of a difference, but changing the square lights to circles, hexagons, or even triangles will give the quilt a different look.

• Use your favorite prints instead of solids, or swap out the solid black for a small scale black-and-white print or another color.

• Add more lights in different sizes along the hanging black strips.

Art and Design Critique

See Principles of Design (page 11).

Balance, movement, and unity all play a role in *Party Lights*. Movement is created by the wavy lines and having the squares offset at the end of them. The wavy lines give the impression of the squares blowing gently in the breeze. The unified shapes and sizes of the lights create a balanced design.

Hexi Network

Finished quilt: 17″ × 41″

A die cutter will make cutting all the hexagons and circles for this project easy, but if you don't have one available to you, just cut the shapes by hand, using the hexagon patterns (page 59) to make templates. Don't get too hung up on trying to exactly replicate the colors and layout that I used. Use the directions provided as a guideline to create your own version, using the colors and placement that you like. I think this quilt would be great done using batiks or a combination of small scale prints and solids.

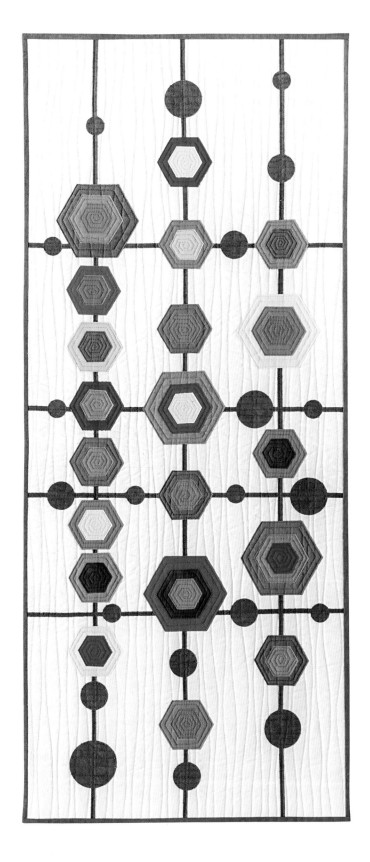

Materials

FABRICS

White: 18″ × 42″

Dark gray: 45″ wide, ½ yard

Assorted colors: 1 fat quarter (18″ × 20″)
in *each* of 7 colors for hexagons

Wool felt: 18″ × 42″
(see The Middle Layer, page 36)

Backing for false back (optional): 17″ × 41″
(see Tip: False Backs, page 42)

OTHER SUPPLIES AND TOOLS

Fusible web: 1 package 10 yards × 20″
(I prefer Mistyfuse.)

Pressing sheet: Your choice
(see Pressing Sheets, page 34)

Muslin (optional): 18″ × 42″
(see Construct the Base, page 56)

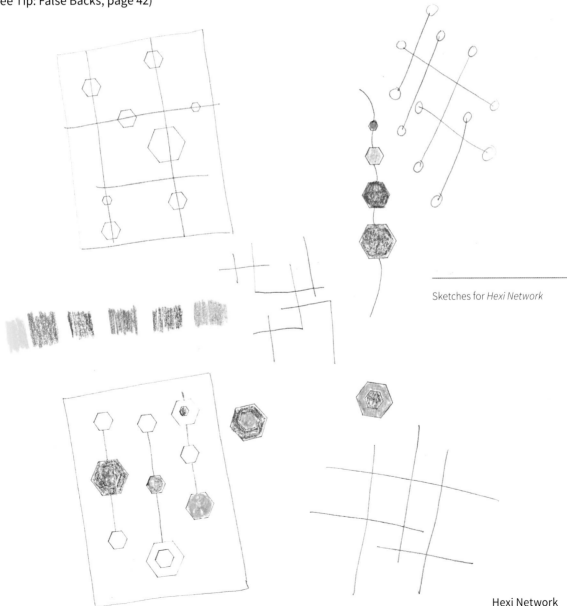

Sketches for *Hexi Network*

CONSTRUCT THE BASE

See Fusing Basics (page 38).

Note: Putting a layer of muslin on the back side of the wool felt is optional, but I never skip this step; for quilts that will be hung on the wall, the muslin adds a bit of body and helps the quilt hang flat and straight.

1. Fuse the muslin to one side of the wool felt.

   This is a great time to use up any scraps of fusible web instead of using full widths. The object is to just adhere the muslin to the wool felt enough so that it doesn't shift when quilting. Place scraps of fusible web about 6″ apart across the surface of the wool felt, cover with a pressing sheet, and press with a hot iron. Remove the pressing sheet, place the muslin on top of the wool felt, and press with a hot iron to fuse it together.

2. Fuse the white 18″ × 42″ piece to the other side of the wool felt.

3. Quilt the white background using wavy vertical lines randomly spaced ½″–¾″ apart across the surface (see Quilt-As-You-Go, page 42).

4. Trim the quilt to 17″ × 41″.

CREATE THE GRID

1. From the dark gray fabric, cut 3 pieces 2″ × 45″ and set them aside to use later for the binding.

2. Fuse a layer of fusible web to the wrong side of the remaining dark gray fabric. Cut 3 strips ¼″ × 45″ and 4 strips ¼″ × 17″.

3. Place the 3 longer strips on the quilt from short edge to short edge, spacing them randomly apart, and iron to fuse them in place.

4. Place the 4 shorter strips on the quilt from long edge to long edge, spacing them randomly apart, and iron to fuse them in place. *Fig. A*

ADD THE HEXAGONS

Important: *Before cutting the following pieces, fuse a layer of fusible web to the wrong side of each piece of fabric.*

1. Cut 5 large hexagons from 5 different colored fabrics and place them randomly on the grid lines (see hexagon patterns, page 59). *Fig. B*

2. Cut several medium hexagons from the colored fabric and place them randomly on the grid. Place a medium hexagon on each of the large hexagons already on the grid lines. *Fig. C*

3. Cut several small hexagons from the colored fabric and place them randomly on the grid. Place a small hexagon on each of the large hexagons already on the grid lines.

4. Cut several circles of different sizes from the dark gray fabric and place them randomly on the grid lines (see circle patterns, page 59). *Fig. D*

5. Iron to fuse all the hexagons and circles in place.

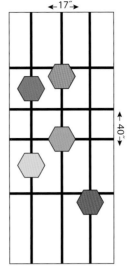

A. Place the strips vertically and horizontally, spacing them randomly.

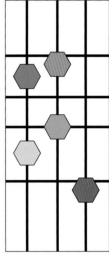

B. Place the 5 large hexagons on the grid.

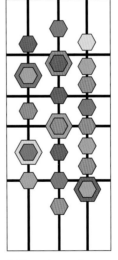

C. Place the medium hexagons on the grid.

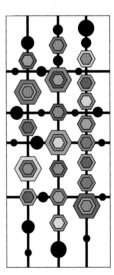

D. Place the small hexagons and the circles on the grid.

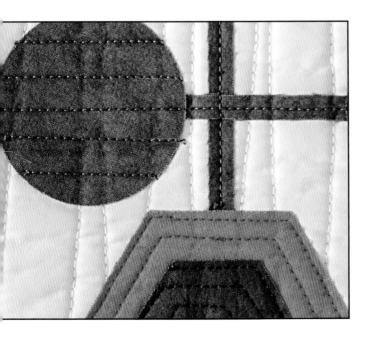

Make It Your Own

- Use wavy lines instead of straight ones to connect the hexagons, or change the shape of the quilt to a hexagon shape instead of a rectangle.

- Use a buttonhole stitch around the edges of the hexagons.

- Limit your color palette for the hexagons to just three colors or use your favorite prints.

Art and Design Critique

See Principles of Design (page 11).

Hexi Network uses just two shapes, and it's the variety of those shapes that keep this quilt from reading as flat or boring. The use of the white background contrasts with the dark gray used for the lines that create the grid that connects the hexagon shapes together. The lines contribute to the sense of movement in that they encourage the eye to follow them moving from one hexi to the next searching for a place to rest.

QUILT AND BIND

1. Quilt the hexagons and circles.

2. With dark gray thread in the top of the sewing machine, stitch down the center of all the dark gray grid lines.

3. Fuse the false back fabric to the back side of the quilt.

4. Bind the quilt using the 3 dark gray 2″ × 45″ strips and either my method Four-Step Binding (page 44) or your favorite binding technique. Cut 1 strip in half crosswise to bind the 2 short edges of the quilt.

5. Add a label and a hanging sleeve (page 46) to the back of the quilt.

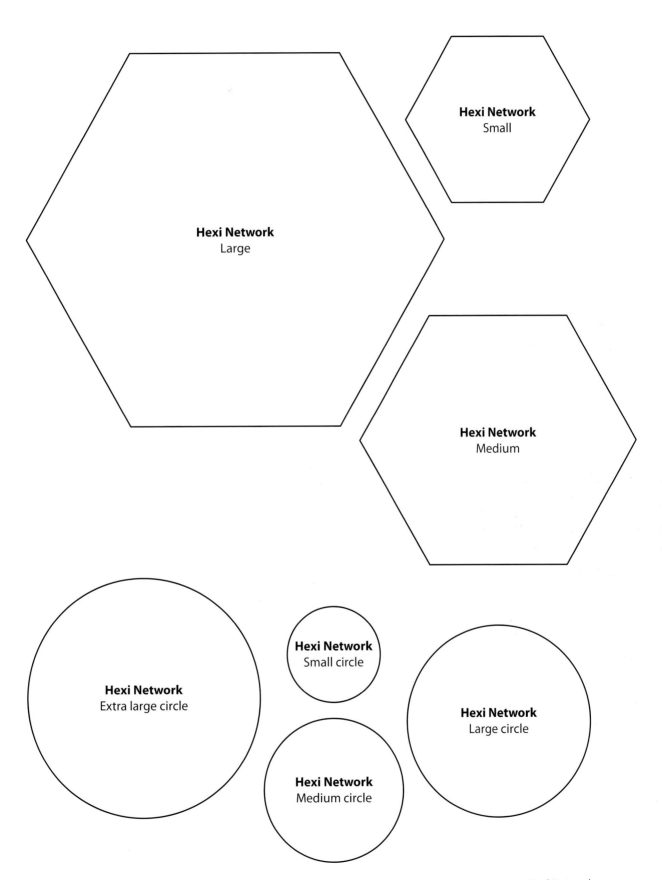

Hexi Network
Large

Hexi Network
Small

Hexi Network
Medium

Hexi Network
Extra large circle

Hexi Network
Small circle

Hexi Network
Medium circle

Hexi Network
Large circle

Waves

Finished quilt: 16˝ × 18˝

Creating a quilt using interlocking curved edges is a snap when you use fusing as the construction method. Just take care that the edges of the pieces are placed right next to each other before fusing them in place so that the background doesn't show through any gaps. You can approach creating the waves in two ways, and I've provided directions for both, so you can choose the one that appeals to you.

Materials

FABRICS

Assorted colors: 1 fat quarter (18″ × 20″) in *each* of these 7 colors: white, pink, purple, yellow, orange, blue, green

Black-and-white print: 10″ × 20″ for binding

Wool felt: 17″ × 18″
(see The Middle Layer, page 36)

Backing for false back (optional): 16″ × 18″
(see Tip: False Backs, page 42)

OTHER SUPPLIES AND TOOLS

Fusible web: 1 package 10 yards × 20″
(I prefer Mistyfuse.)

Pressing sheet: Your choice
(see Pressing Sheets, page 34)

Muslin (optional): 17″ × 19″
(see Construct the Base, page 62)

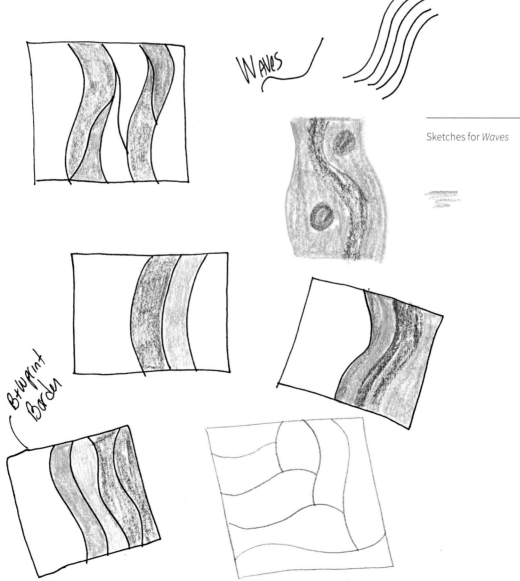

Sketches for *Waves*

CONSTRUCT THE BASE

See Fusing Basics (page 38).

Note: Putting a layer of muslin on the back side of the wool felt is optional, but I never skip this step; for quilts that will be hung on the wall, the muslin adds a bit of body and helps the quilt hang flat and straight.

1. Fuse the muslin to one side of the wool felt.

   This is a great time to use up any scraps of fusible web instead of using full widths. The object is to just adhere the muslin to the wool felt enough so that it doesn't shift when quilting. Place scraps of fusible web about 6″ apart across the surface of the wool felt, cover with a pressing sheet, and press with a hot iron. Remove the pressing sheet, place the muslin on top of the wool felt, and press with a hot iron to fuse it together.

2. Fuse the white 17″ × 19″ piece to the other side of the wool felt.

CREATE THE WAVES

Important: *Before cutting the following pieces, fuse a layer of fusible web to the wrong side of each piece of fabric.*

1. Place the pink fabric on the cutting surface right side up. Put the purple fabric on top right side up. Using a rotary cutter, free-form cut a random wavy line along the 20″ edge. *Fig. A*

   Place the pink fabric on the quilt along the right 19″ edge. (Save the same-shaped purple piece that you just cut for another project. You will not be using it for this one.) *Fig. B*

2. Place the yellow fabric on the cutting surface right side up. Put the rest of the purple fabric that has the wave edge on top right side up. Using a rotary cutter, free-form cut a random wavy line along the 20″ edge. *Fig. C*

   Place the purple piece on the quilt along edge of the pink piece. (Save the yellow piece that you just cut for another project. You will not be using it for this one.) *Fig. D*

3. Place the orange fabric on the cutting surface right side up. Put the rest of the yellow fabric that has the wave edge on top right side up. Using a rotary cutter free-form cut a random wavy line along the 20″ edge.

   Place the yellow piece on the quilt along edge of the purple piece. (Save the orange piece that you just cut for another project. You will not be using it for this one.)

4. Place the blue fabric on the cutting surface right side up. Put the rest of the orange fabric that has the wave edge on top right side up. Using a rotary cutter free-form cut a random wavy line along the 20″ edge.

   Place the orange piece on the quilt along edge of the yellow piece. (Save the blue piece that you just cut for another project. You will not be using it for this one.)

5. Place the green fabric on the cutting surface right side up. Put the rest of the blue fabric that has the wave edge on top right side up. Using a rotary cutter free-form cut a random wavy line along the 20˝ edge.

Place the blue piece on the quilt along edge of the orange piece. (Save the green piece that you just cut for another project. You will not be using it for this one.)

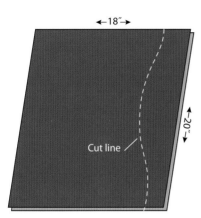

A. Cut a random wavy line.

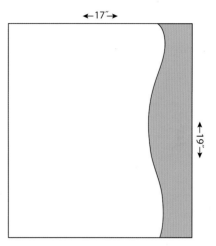

B. Place the pink wave on the quilt along the right edge.

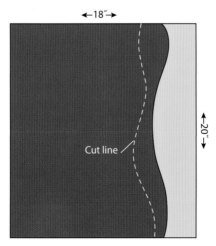

C. Place the purple fabric on the top of the yellow fabric and cut a wavy line.

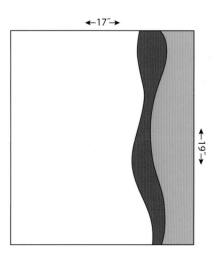

D. Place the purple wave on the quilt along the right edge.

Waves

6. Put the rest of the green fabric that has the wave edge on the cutting mat right side up. Using a rotary cutter free-form cut a random wavy line along the 20″ edge. Place the green piece on the quilt along edge of the blue piece.

7. Make sure the pieces are placed close enough together so that the white fabric beneath isn't visible. Fuse them in place. *Fig. E*

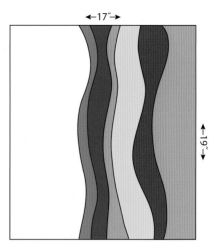

E. Fuse all the waves in place.

Another Approach

This alternative method for creating the wave pieces works just as well as the cut-and-place method, and it doesn't create as much waste. The only drawback is that you must make sure that your cuts along the traced lines are exact; otherwise, you may end up with gaps that allow the white fabric below to show through.

Cut a piece of craft paper 17″ × 19″. Use a black marker to draw 6 random wavy lines along the right 19″ edge. Cut the craft paper apart along the drawn lines and use these as templates to cut the pieces from your fabric. Then place them on the quilt and fuse them in place.

QUILT THE WAVES

1. Quilt the waves, using the shape of the waves to guide your stitching lines.

2. Quilt the white area of the quilt.

FINISH THE QUILT

1. Cut 4 strips 2″ × 20 from the black-and-white print and set them aside to use for the binding.

2. Fuse a layer of fusible web to the remaining piece of black-and-white print fabric. Cut a strip ⅛″ × 20″ from it and fuse it in place along the edge of the green fabric.

3. Fuse the false back fabric to the back side of the quilt and trim the quilt to 16″ × 18″.

4. Bind the quilt using the 4 black-and-white 2″ × 20″ strips and either my method Four-Step Binding (page 44) or your favorite binding technique.

3. Add a label and a hanging sleeve (page 46) to the back of the quilt.

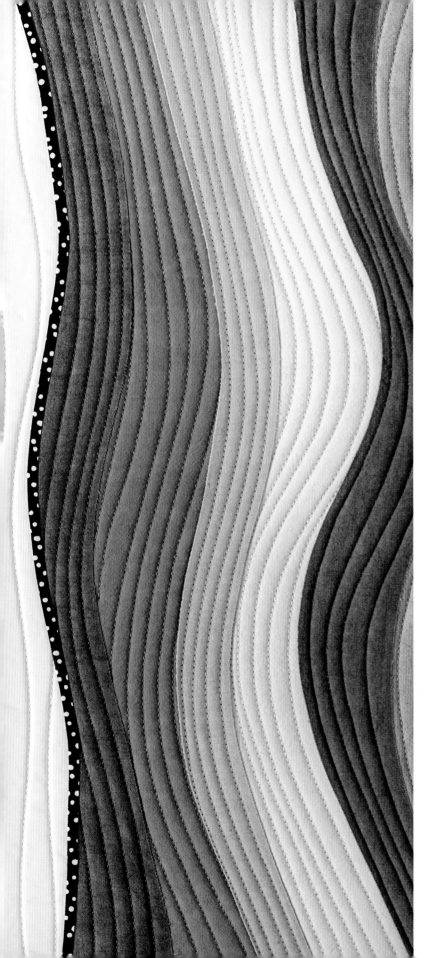

Make It Your Own

• Instead of leaving white space, carry the waves all the way from edge to edge.

• Use this design as a jumping-off point for a larger quilt. Create several wave blocks and sew them together using ¼″ seams rotating the blocks as you sew them together.

• Add some appliqué circle shapes in the white space area, or leave some white space in-between some of the waves.

Art and Design Critique

See Principles of Design (page 11).

Movement is a strong design element in *Waves* and is created by the use of the wavy offset colored shapes and the quilting lines. The black-and-white stripe line that separates the colored waves from the white space emphasizes the transition to the white space and gives the eye a break from the waves and a way to transition from one side of the quilt to the other.

Stacks of Three

Finished quilt: 46″ × 26″

Altering the angles of the edges and sides of the rectangles turns a boring shape into an interesting one and helps to create movement in the overall design. The stark white background of this quilt provides a high level of contrast and makes it seem as if the red is dancing across the surface. Red is one of my favorite colors to use with gray, but any bright saturated color will work well here, so feel free to swap it out for your favorite instead.

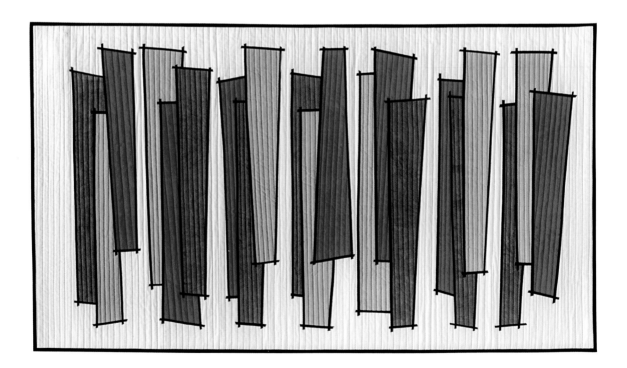

Materials

FABRICS

White: 48″ × 28″

Dark gray: ½ yard

Light gray: ½ yard

Red: ½ yard

Black: 1⅜ yards (You will have fabric left over for another project.)

Wool felt: 48″ × 28″
(see The Middle Layer, page 36)

Backing for false back (optional):
48″ × 28″ (see Tip: False Backs, page 42)

OTHER SUPPLIES AND TOOLS

Fusible web: 1 package 10 yards × 20″
(I prefer Mistyfuse.)

Pressing sheet: Your choice
(see Pressing Sheets, page 34)

Muslin (optional): 28″ × 50″
(see Construct the Base, page 68)

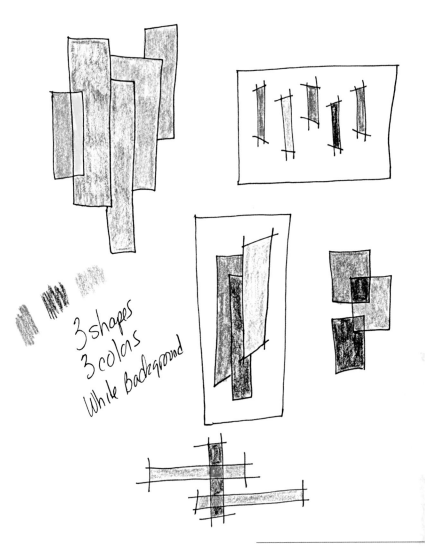

Sketches for *Stacks of Three*

Cutting

Important: *Before cutting the following pieces, fuse a layer of fusible web to the wrong side of each piece of fabric (see Fusing Basics, page 38).*

Dark gray: Cut 7 rectangles 18″ × 3″.

Light gray: Cut 7 rectangles 18″ × 3″.

Red: Cut 7 rectangles 18″ × 3″.

Angle the sides and the top and bottom short edges of each rectangle. Don't be concerned with making each shape the same. Making your angle cuts random will result in a more interesting finished quilt.

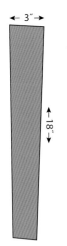

← 3″ →

↕ 18″

Angle the top
and bottom
short edges of
each rectangle.

CONSTRUCT THE BASE

Note: Putting a layer of muslin on the back side of the wool felt is optional, but I never skip this step, because for quilts that will be hung on the wall, it adds a bit of body and helps the quilt hang flat and straight.

1. Fuse the muslin to one side of the wool felt.

   This is a great time to use up any scraps of fusible web instead of using full widths. The object is to just adhere the muslin to the wool felt enough so that it doesn't shift when quilting. Place scraps of fusible web about 6″ apart across the surface of the wool felt, cover with a pressing sheet, and press with a hot iron. Remove the pressing sheet, place the muslin on top of the wool felt, and press with a hot iron to fuse it together.

2. Fuse the white 48″ × 28″ piece to the other side of the wool felt.

3. Quilt the white background using vertical lines randomly spaced ½″–¾″ apart across the surface (see Quilt-As-You-Go, page 42).

ADD THE RECTANGLE APPLIQUÉ PIECES

1. Although it may look as if the color placement in the stacks is random, there is actually a predetermined format.

   a. Starting from the left side of the quilt, place the first layer of each stack on the quilt in the following order:

      Dark gray ▶ Light gray ▶ Red ▶ Dark gray ▶ Light gray ▶ Red ▶ Dark gray

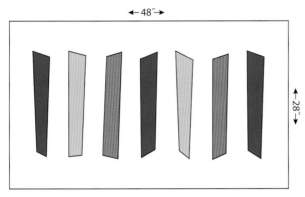

Place the first layer of the stacks on the quilt.

   b. Add the second layer to each stack, overlapping the first piece and offsetting this second piece in the stack.

   c. Starting from the left side of the quilt, place the second layer of each stack on the quilt in the following order:

      Light gray ▶ Red ▶ Dark gray ▶ Light gray ▶ Red ▶ Dark gray ▶ Light gray

   d. Add the third and final layer to each stack, overlapping the second piece and offsetting this third piece in the stack.

   e. Starting from the left side of the quilt, place the third layer of each stack on the quilt in the following order:

      Red ▶ Dark gray ▶ Light gray ▶ Red ▶ Dark gray ▶ Light gray ▶ Red

2. Before fusing the stacks in place on the background, make sure you are pleased with the placement—take the time to shift the rectangles so that each color is visible in each stack. When you are happy with the placement of the stacks, press with a hot iron to fuse them in place.

3. Quilt the stacks using vertical lines spaced ½″–¾″ apart.

ADD THE BLACK OUTLINES

1. Cut 4 strips 2″ × 46″ for the binding along the length of the fabric and set them aside.

2. Fuse a layer of fusible web to the wrong side of the rest of the black fabric.

3. Using a rotary cutter and ruler, cut strips ranging from ¼″ to ½″ wide from the black fabric along the long edge. The varying widths will add to the dynamic visual appeal of the quilt.

4. Fuse the strips along the raw edge of each appliqué shape, letting the black strips extend a little beyond the edge of each shape.

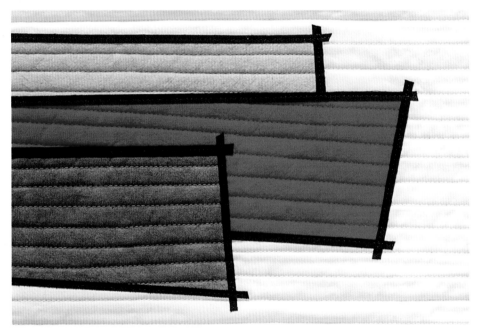

Let the black strips extend a little beyond the edge of each shape.

5. With black thread in the top of the sewing machine, stitch down the center of all the black lines.

FINISH THE QUILT

1. Fuse the false back fabric to the back side of the quilt and trim the quilt to 46″ × 26″.

2. Bind the quilt using the 4 black 2″ × 46″ strips and either my method Four-Step Binding (page 44) or your favorite binding technique.

3. Add a label and a hanging sleeve (page 46) to the back of the quilt.

Make It Your Own

- Swap out the red for your favorite print.

- Add a small appliqué circle here and there on the stack appliqué pieces.

- Instead of using a solid piece of fabric for each shape in the stack, create strip fabric using the technique described in *Going in Circles* (page 75).

Art and Design Critique

See Principles of Design (page 11).

Stacks of Three combines shape, color, and value with balance, pattern, and unity. The limited color palette allows the emphasis to be on the stark contrast between the white background and the stacks; the bold use of red encourages the eye to dance from stack to stack. At first glance, the stacks seem randomly placed, but by repeating the number used, the color combination and the shapes, balance, pattern, and unity are created.

Going in Circles

Finished quilt: 43″ × 57″

Circles are a snap to work with when you use fusing as your construction technique. This quilt comes together very quickly as a fun weekend project. I used solids for my version, but it would also look great done with a combination of solids and prints. Make a kids' version using novelty prints or a more sophisticated one using batiks.

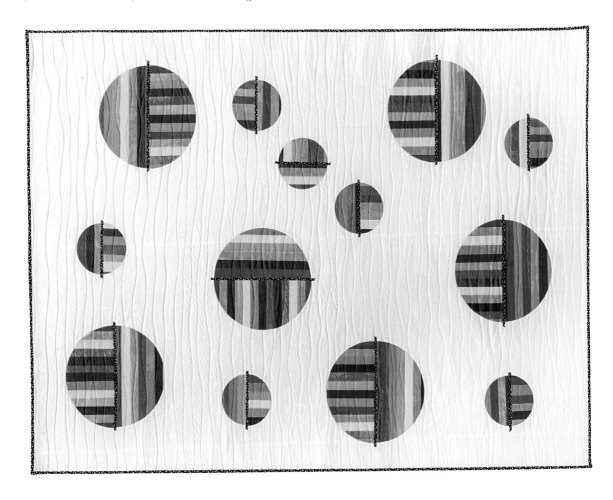

Materials

FABRICS

White: 1¾ yards, at least 45″ wide

Black-and-white print: ½ yard

Assorted colors: 1 fat quarter
(18″ × 22″) in *each* of 6–9 colors

Wool felt: 45″ × 60″
(see The Middle Layer, page 36)

Backing for false back (optional):
1¾ yards, at least 45″ wide
(see Tip: False Backs, page 42)

OTHER SUPPLIES AND TOOLS

Fusible web: 1 package
10 yards × 20″ (I prefer Mistyfuse.)

Pressing sheet: Your choice
(see Pressing Sheets, page 34)

Muslin (optional): 45″ × 60″
(see Construct the Base, page 74)

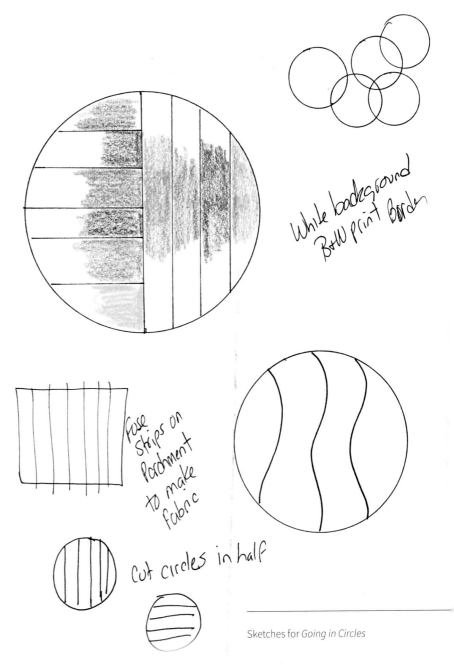

White background
B+W print Border

Fuse strips on
Parchment to make
fabric

Cut circles in half

Sketches for *Going in Circles*

CONSTRUCT THE BASE

See Fusing Basics (page 38).

Note: Putting a layer of muslin on the back side of the wool felt is optional, but I never skip this step; for quilts that will be hung on the wall, the muslin adds a bit of body and helps the quilt hang flat and straight.

1. Fuse the muslin to one side of the wool felt.

   This is a great time to use up any scraps of fusible web instead of using full widths. The object is to just adhere the muslin to the wool felt enough so that it doesn't shift when quilting. Place scraps of fusible web about 6″ apart across the surface of the wool felt, cover with a pressing sheet, and press with a hot iron. Remove the pressing sheet, place the muslin on top of the wool felt, and press with a hot iron to fuse it together.

2. Fuse the white fabric piece to the other side of the wool felt and trim off any excess.

CREATE THE STRIP FABRIC

The circles for this quilt are cut from fabric that is made up of overlapping 1″-wide strips.

Important: *Before cutting the following pieces, fuse a layer of fusible web to the wrong side of each piece of fabric.*

1. Cut 6 strips 1″ × 22″ from each of the colored fabrics. Note that you may need more strips than this depending on how many circles you want to put on your quilt. Start with 6 strips and cut more if you need them.

2. Arrange the strips on the pressing sheet, alternating the colors and overlapping them approximately ⅛″ along the long edge to create a larger piece of fabric.

Overlap ⅛″. ↘	Strip 3
	Strip 2
Overlap ⅛″. ↗	Strip 1

Overlap the strips ⅛″.

TIP // Press, Don't Iron!

Rather than waiting until all the strips are laid in place to fuse them together, press them after placing 3 or 4 strips. Use a pressing motion instead of an ironing one to keep the strips from shifting out of place. Lift the iron up and down rather than sliding it across the surface of the strips.

MAKE THE CIRCLES

For this quilt, I used 5″ and 10″ circles, but the circle size(s) you use for this project is not critical, and you can create your quilt using any size and combination of circles you like. If you don't have access to a die cutter to cut the circles, then take a look around the house for round-shaped objects you can trace, such as dinner plates, coffee mugs, or plastic container lids.

1. Cut 8 circles about 5″ in diameter, using the *Flower Power* pattern (page 93) from the strip fabric you created (see Create the Strip Fabric, page 74).

2. Create a circle pattern about 10″ in diameter, using a plate or other round object and use it to cut 6 circles from the strip fabric.

3. From the 10″ circles, cut 3 in half with the strips running vertically and 3 with the stripes running horizontally. *Fig. A*

4. From the 5″ circles, cut 4 in half with the strips running vertically and 4 with the stripes running horizontally.

5. Arrange the circles on the quilt top, pairing a half-circle with the strips running horizontally with one running vertically. When you are happy with the placement, press them with a hot iron to fuse them in place. You will have enough half-circles to make 8 of the 5″ circles, but I chose to make only 7 of them. You can save the extra pieces for another project. *Fig. B*

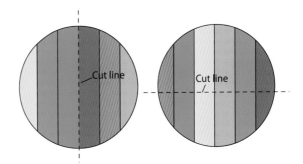

A. Cut half of the circles with the strips running horizontally and the other half with them running vertically.

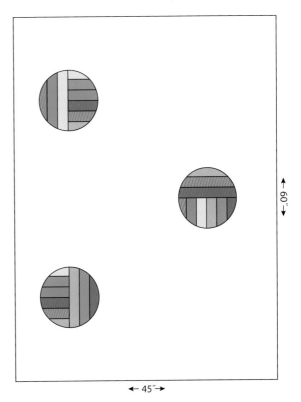

B. Arrange the circles on the quilt top pairing a half-circle with the strips running horizontally with one running vertically.

QUILT THE TOP

Quilt the top using wavy lines that extend from the top long edge to the bottom long edge. I used Superior Threads MonoPoly in both the top and bottom of the machine to quilt the top (see Quilt-As-You-Go, page 42).

FINISH THE QUILT

1. From the black-and-white fabric, cut 6 strips 2″ × width of fabric and set them aside to use for the binding.

2. Fuse a layer of fusible web to the wrong side the remaining piece of black-and-white fabric. Cut 4 strips ¼″ × width of fabric. Fuse a strip of the black-and-white fabric along the center edge of each circle where the horizontal and the vertical sides meet, letting the strip extend beyond the edge of the circle.

Let the strip extend beyond the edge of the circle.

3. With the thread color of your choice in the machine, sew down the center of each black-and-white strip.

4. Fuse the false back fabric to the back side of the quilt and trim the quilt to 43″ × 57″

5. Bind the quilt using either my method Four-Step Binding (page 44) or your favorite binding technique.

6. Add a label and a hanging sleeve (page 46) to the back of the quilt.

Make It Your Own

- This technique will work for squares, rectangles, or just about any other shape you can think of.

- Outline each circle in the black-and-white print, using the cookie cutter method used to create the outlined circle in *Flower Power* (page 88).

- Instead of using striped fabric for both sides of the circle, use a solid for one side

Art and Design Critique

See Principles of Design (page 11).

Balance and movement are on display here. Although the circles are randomly placed across the surface, the number and placement results in a balanced design because there are no large gaps between them. The configuration of the circles also plays an important role in encouraging the eye to travel around the quilt. If the circles were placed with the centers (the black-and-white strips) running in the same direction, the resulting design wouldn't be nearly as visually engaging.

Going in Circles

Inside Out

Finished quilt: 54″ × 60″

This quilt won first place in the appliqué category at QuiltCon 2017 and is a perfect example of how using simple shapes combined with a minimal amount of color doesn't necessarily result in a boring quilt. The white panel in the middle provides balance to the outer gray panels while at the same time lends contrast to the overall color scheme. That combined with the simple geometric shapes results in a visually exciting and dynamic quilt.

It's easy to size this quilt up or down to suit your needs by starting with a larger or smaller piece of paper; just keep the width of the three sections the same.

Materials

FABRICS

White: 1¾ yards

Light gray: 1¾ yards

Dark gray: 1¾ yards

Black for binding: 4 strips 2″ × 65″

Black for outlining: ¼ yard plus 1 strip 6″ × 60″

Wool felt: 62″ × 68″ (see The Middle Layer, page 36)

Backing for false back (optional): 62″ × 68″
(see Tip: False Backs, page 42)

OTHER SUPPLIES AND TOOLS

Craft paper: 54″ × 60″

Straight edge ruler

Black marker

Tracing paper

Fusible web: 1 package 10 yards × 20″
and 1 package 2½ yards × 20″
(I prefer Mistyfuse.)

Pressing sheet: Your choice
(see Pressing Sheets, page 34)

Muslin (optional): 62″ × 68″
(see Construct the Base, page 81)

TIP // Using Craft Paper

If you can't find craft paper in the size you need, just tape several pieces together using clear tape to create a larger piece of paper to draw your quilt pattern on.

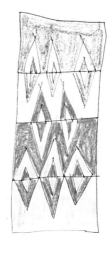

Sketches for Inside Out

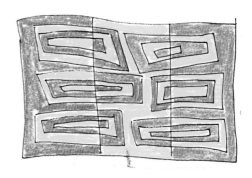

Inside Out

Cutting

Important: *Before cutting the any fabric, fuse a layer of fusible web to the wrong side of each piece of fabric (see Fusing Basics, page 38).*

White: Cut 1 piece 18˝ × 60˝.

Light gray: Cut 1 piece 18˝ × 60˝.

Dark gray: Cut 1 piece 18˝ × 60˝.

TIP // Washable Quilts

If you are planning on washing and using your finished quilt instead of displaying it on the wall, here are a few things to consider:

• Use your favorite quilt batting in place of the wool felt. Wool felt shrinks and stiffens quite a bit when washed and won't have much drape.

• Don't add a layer of muslin to the back of the quilt when constructing the base. Use your chosen quilt back fabric instead and skip the addition of the false back. Using both the muslin and the false back will add stiffness to the finished quilt which may not be desirable for a functional quilt.

• Consider waiting until the quilt top is finished before you add any quilting instead of using my method in Quilt-As-You-Go (page 42). The additional layers of stitching could add stiffness that may be undesirable in a functional quilt.

CREATE A DESIGN

1. Divide the craft paper into 3 vertical sections each 18˝ × 60˝. *Fig. A*

2. Working in the center area only, draw random geometric shapes along both outer edges, keeping the shapes random and offset from one another. The goal is to create organic shapes that are all different from one another in size and shape. Work from side to side rather than drawing all the shapes on one side and then the other. When you work from side to side the finished drawing will appear more random. *Fig. B*

3. Number the shapes and trace each shape on tracing paper to make a template. *Fig. C*

CONSTRUCT THE BASE

1. Fuse the muslin (if you're using it) to one side of the wool felt.

   This is a great time to use up any scraps of fusible web instead of using full widths. The object is to just adhere the muslin to the wool felt enough so that it doesn't shift when quilting. Place scraps of fusible web about 6″ apart across the surface of the wool felt, cover a pressing sheet, and press with a hot iron. Remove the pressing sheet, place the muslin on top of the wool felt, and press with a hot iron to fuse it together.

2. Fuse the white, light gray, and dark gray 18″ × 60″ pieces to the other side of the wool felt, placing the white in the center. *Fig. D*

3. Quilt the top using random lines spaced ½″–¾″ apart on each section. Alter the angle of the line in each section to create additional visual interest, or if you prefer, quilt the top using your favorite quilting method (see Quilt-As-You-Go, page 42).

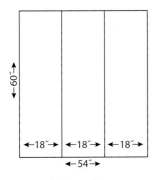

A. Divide the craft paper into 3 sections.

B. Draw random shapes in the center area only.

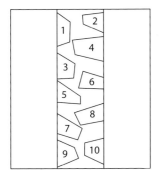

C. Number the shapes.

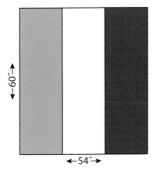

D. Place the white fabric in the middle.

CUT AND FUSE THE APPLIQUÉ SHAPES

Each numbered shape is cut from the white fabric and the corresponding gray fabric depending on which side of the quilt you're working on.

1. For the first shape ("1" in the drawing), cut a piece of white fabric and light gray fabric each a little larger than the shape you need to cut, and put them right sides together on the cutting surface. Place the tracing paper template on top and using either a rotary cutter and ruler or scissors, cut the shape out along the traced line. This forms the base shape to work from. *Fig. E*

2. With the base shape pieces still right sides together, use a rotary cutter and ruler (or scissors) to cut another shape from inside of these. You can make the cuts random or use a chalk marker to mark cutting lines to use as a guide. Set the secondary shapes you just cut aside. Place the base shapes that now have the insides cut from them on the quilt top in the appropriate place. *Fig. F*

3. Trim ½″ off each edge of the secondary shapes that were created in Step 2. With the shapes right sides together use a rotary cutter and ruler to cut another shape from inside of these. Set the new shapes aside and place the pieces that now have the insides cut from them on the quilt top in the appropriate place. *Fig. G*

4. Trim ½″–¾″ off each edge from the remaining shapes and place them on the quilt top in the appropriate place. *Fig. H*

5. Press the shapes with a hot iron to fuse them in place on the quilt top.

6. Repeat this process for all the shapes you drew and traced in Create a Design, Steps 2 and 3 (page 80). After fusing all the pieces in place on the quilt top, quilt each piece using the shape of the piece as the stitching guide.

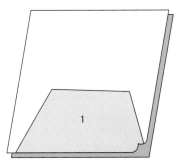

E. With right sides together, cut the first shape from the white and gray fabric.

Cut secondary shape.

F. Cut a shape from the inside of the base shape.

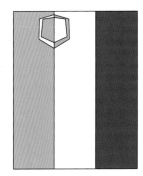

Secondary shape

Trim ½″ all around.

Cut secondary shape.

G. Cut a shape from the inside of the secondary shape.

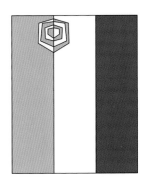

Trim ½″ all around.

H. Cut ½″ off the remaining shapes and place them on the quilt.

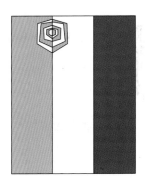

ADD THE OUTLINES

1. Fuse a layer of fusible web to the wrong side of the black outlining fabric.

2. Using a rotary cutter and ruler, cut strips ranging from ¼″ to ½″ wide from the ¼ yard black fabric along the long edge. The varying widths will add to the dynamic visual appeal of the quilt.

3. Fuse the strips along the raw edge of each appliqué shape, letting the black strips extend a little beyond the edge of each shape.

Let the black strips extend beyond the edge of each shape.

4. Cut 2 long strips from the 6″ × 60″ piece and fuse them along the long raw edges between each base color.

5. With black thread in the top of the sewing machine, stitch down the center of all the black lines.

FINISH THE QUILT

1. Fuse the false back fabric to the back side of the quilt and trim the quilt to 54″ × 60″.

2. Bind the quilt using either my method Four-Step Binding (page 44) or your favorite binding technique.

3. Add a label and a hanging sleeve (page 46) to the back of the quilt.

Make It Your Own

- Add a pop of color by using a different color solid for the center shapes.

- Use wavy lines instead of straight ones for the rectangle shapes.

- Use a different shape or combination of shapes such as triangles and circles instead of just rectangles.

Art and Design Critique

See Principles of Design (page 11).

When one line intersects with another, it becomes a shape; when used with a limited color palette with a subtle value shift, a striking graphic design is the result. This design is also a great example of how pattern can be created without the need to duplicate the shapes exactly. The variety of angles and shapes provides complexity to the finished design.

Flower Power

Finished quilt: 44″ × 65″

*The idea for **Flower Power** came to me after I finished making **Inside Out** (page 78). I wanted to do something similar but different so it didn't look like just another version of the first quilt. After playing around with rounding the edges of a rectangle, the petal shape emerged and the idea for the flower-power quilt emerged.*

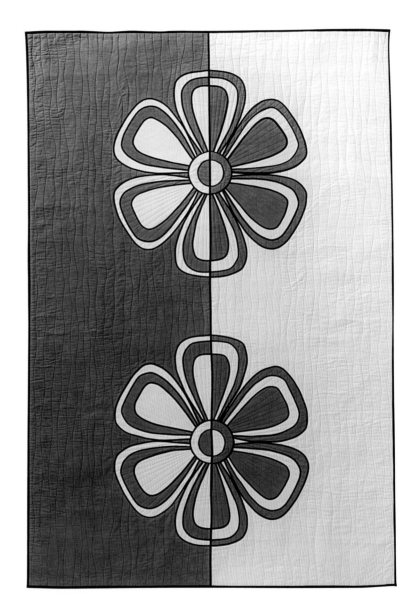

Materials

FABRICS

White: 2 yards

Dark gray: 2 yards

Black for outlines: 45″ × 45″

Black for binding: 4 strips 2″ × 72″

Wool felt: 48″ × 69″
(see The Middle Layer, page 36)

Backing for false back (optional):
48″ × 69″ (see Tip: False Backs,
page 42)

OTHER SUPPLIES AND TOOLS

Fusible web: 1 package 10 yards × 20″
(I prefer Mistyfuse.)

Pressing sheet: Your choice
(see Pressing Sheets, page 34)

Muslin (optional): 48″ × 69″
(see Construct the Base, page 88)

Sketches for *Flower Power*

Flower Power

CONSTRUCT THE BASE

See Fusing Basics (page 38).

Note: If you're planning on washing your quilt, consider using batting in place of the wool felt (see Tip: Washable Quilts, page 80).

1. Remove the selvage from one side of the white and dark gray fabrics, and then cut the white and dark gray fabrics lengthwise to make 2 pieces 22½″ × 69″.

2. Fuse the muslin fabric to one side of the wool felt.

   This is a great time to use up any scraps of fusible web instead of using full widths. The object is to just adhere the backing to the wool felt enough so that it doesn't shift when quilting. Place scraps of fusible web about 6″ apart across the surface of the wool felt, cover with a pressing sheet, and press with a hot iron. Remove the pressing sheet, place the muslin on top of the wool felt, and press with a hot iron to fuse it together.

3. Fuse 1 each of white and dark gray pieces to the other side of the wool felt. *Fig. A*

4. Quilt the top using random wavy lines spaced ½″–¾″ apart on each section, or if you prefer, quilt the top using your favorite quilting method (see Quilt-As-You-Go, page 42).

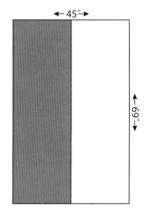

A. Fuse white and dark gray pieces to the wool felt.

CREATE THE FLOWER CENTER CIRCLES

Important: *Before cutting any circles, fuse a layer of fusible web to the wrong side of each piece of fabric.*

In order to get the black outline around the center circles, I developed a technique that I call "cookie cutter outlines." This technique makes it easy to create a border around a circle or an organic, uneven shape.

1. From the black fabric, cut a 7″ × 7″ square. Use the 5″ circle pattern (page 93) to draw a circle on the back side of the black fabric (the side with the fusible web on it). *Fig. B*

2. Using a sharp pair of scissors, cut the circle out of the center of the square, leaving the sides of the square intact. Set the circle that you cut out aside, you won't need it for this project. The other piece is the cookie cutter outline. *Fig. C*

3. Cut a 7″ × 3½″ piece from the white fabric and a 7″ × 3½″ piece from the dark gray fabric.

4. Working on a nonstick surface place the 2 pieces right side up, overlapping the 7″ edge about ⅛″. Press them to fuse them together. Fig. D

5. Put the black circle outline on top of the white and dark gray unit, making sure the centerline is running through the center of the circle. Press to fuse the black cookie cutter outline to the top of the white / dark gray unit. *Fig. E*

6. Trim the fused circle unit down to size, leaving a black border of ⅛″–¼″ all the way around. *Fig. F*

7. Repeat the Steps 1–6 to make another 5″ circle and 2 of the 3″ circles.

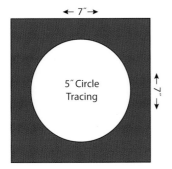

B. Trace the circle on the back side of the black fabric.

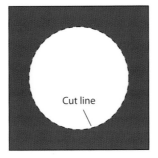

C. Cut out the circle of the center of the square leaving the sides of the square intact.

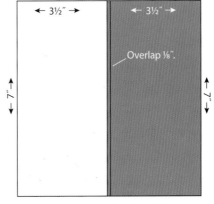

D. Overlap the pieces by ⅛″ and fuse them together.

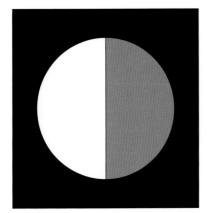

E. Put the black circle outline on top of the white and dark gray unit and fuse it in place.

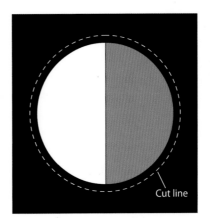

F. Trim the fused circle unit down to size.

CUT OUT THE FLOWER PETALS

Important: *Before cutting any petals, fuse a layer of fusible web to the wrong side of each piece of fabric.*

1. Cut 6 small, 6 medium, and 6 large petals from the white fabric, using the *Flower Power* petal patterns (pages 94 and 95).

2. Cut 6 small, 6 medium, and 6 large petals from the dark gray fabric.

3. Place 1 small white petal and 1 small dark gray petal right sides together on the cutting surface, aligning their edges.

4. Use a rotary cutter and ruler to cut the petals in half. *Fig. G*

5. Repeat Steps 3 and 4 with another pair of small petals, 2 pairs of medium petals, and 2 pairs of large petals.

CREATE THE FLOWERS

1. Trim the quilt base to 45″ × 65″.

2. Place a large circle 17″ from the top edge and another 17″ from the bottom edge of the quilt. *Do not* fuse them in place. You will just be using them as a guide for placing the petals for now. *Fig. H*

3. Place a large white half-petal and a large dark gray half-petal along the centerline of the quilt at the top and bottom of each circle. Place the dark gray half-petals on the white side and the white half-petals on the dark gray side. Place the ends of the petals just under the edges of the circles. *Fig. I*

4. Place the 4 large dark gray petals on the white side of the quilt and the 4 large white petals on the dark gray side of the quilt. Make sure that the end of each petal is just under the edge of the circle. *Fig. J*

5. Layer the medium and small half-petals on top of the large half-petals you've already placed on the quilt top, alternating the colors. Place the ends of the petals just under the edges of the circles. *Fig. K*

6. Layer the medium and small petals on top of the large petals you've already placed on the quilt top, alternating the colors. Place the ends of the petals just under the edges of the circles.

7. Remove the circles and fuse all the petals in place.

8. Quilt the petals.

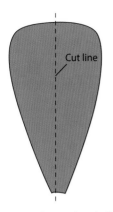

G. Cut the petals in half.

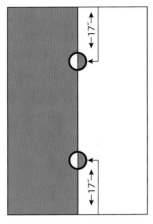

H. Place the large circles on the quilt as a guide.

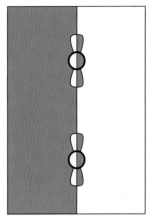

I. Place the large half-petals on the quilt top.

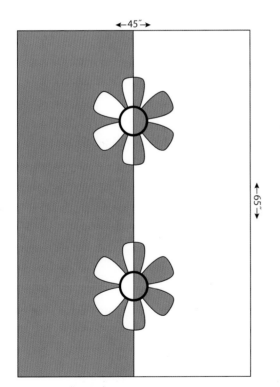

J. Place the large petals on the quilt top.

K. Add the medium and small half-petals on top of the large ones

Flower Power

ADD THE OUTLINES

1. Fuse a layer of fusible web to the wrong side of the black outlining fabric.

2. To make it easier to accommodate the curve around the edge of the petals, cut the black strips for outlining on the bias edge of the fabric. To find the bias edge, lay the fabric flat on the cutting surface. Take one corner of the fabric and fold it diagonally to the opposite corner to create a triangle. The folded edge is the bias edge and that's the edge you should cut your strips from.

   Using a rotary cutter and ruler, cut strips approximately ¼˝ wide from the black fabric along the bias edge. There's no need to make every strip the exact same width, as the varying widths will add to the dynamic visual appeal of the quilt.

   Set aside your longest strip (about 65˝ long) to use at the end.

3. Fuse the strips along the raw edge of each petal shape.

4. Place the large circles on the quilt top. Place them so that the white side of the circle is on the dark gray side. Place a small circle on top of the large one making sure that the white side of the small circle is on the dark gray side of the large circle. Fuse the circles in place.

5. Take the long strip that you set aside earlier and place it down the center of the quilt from top to bottom. Fuse the strip in place.

6. With black thread in the top of the sewing machine, stitch down the center of all the black lines.

FINISH THE QUILT

1. Bind the quilt using either my method Four-Step Binding (page 44) or your favorite binding technique.

2. Add a label and a hanging sleeve (page 46) to the back of the quilt.

Make It Your Own

• When I originally sketched ideas for the design for this quilt, I added a wavy line with leaves on either side, down the edge of the sides of the quilt. Layer the leaves the same way you did the flower petals.

• Change up the colors and use a combination of brights or even prints instead of gray and white.

• Alter the shape of the petals or add another layer of petals behind them.

My original *Flower Power* sketch

Flower Power
5″ circle

Flower Power
3″ circle

Art and Design Critique

See Principles of Design (page 11).

Like *Inside Out* (page 78), *Flower Power* is a great example of how, when used effectively, contrast itself can result in a striking graphic design. The simplicity of the imagery in this quilt reinforces the impact of the contrast to the eye. Although there's a lot of empty space in the quilt, the scale of the flowers creates an overall balanced design.

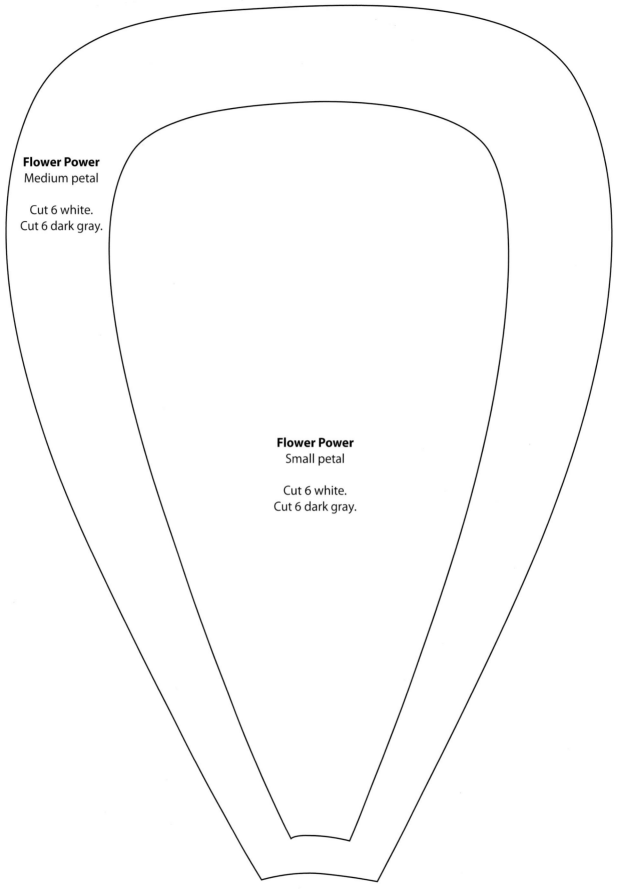

Flower Power
Medium petal

Cut 6 white.
Cut 6 dark gray.

Flower Power
Small petal

Cut 6 white.
Cut 6 dark gray.

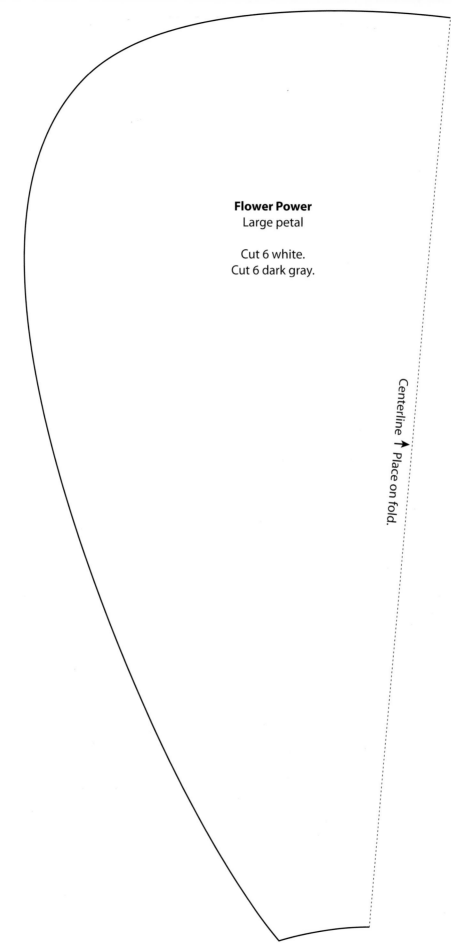

Flower Power
Large petal

Cut 6 white.
Cut 6 dark gray.

Centerline → Place on fold.

WHAT'S NEXT

Critique, Learn, and Develop Your Personal Style

WHAT IS PERSONAL STYLE?

One of the questions I get asked the most by my students is, "How do I develop my own personal style?" Before I answer, I think it's helpful to understand what it means to have a personal style or *visual voice*, as I also like to call it.

Connect the Boxes, 40˝ × 40˝

I define visual voice as *the intuitive or instinctual nature that drives an artist to use the techniques, colors, or materials to create a piece of work that is somehow connected to the artist's previous work*. It's what motivates the artist to work without forethought and without relying on serendipity for the result. It can only be achieved (1) with a mastery of the techniques used and (2) if the influence of styles of teachers and other artists is not present in the results. To find it, artists must have passion for their craft so that they are compelled to push forward, practice, and learn from their mistakes. You cannot "dabble" in techniques and expect to find it. It takes study, hard work, focus, and practice. You can't decide on a Friday evening that you're going to work on developing a personal style and expect to find it by Monday morning!

So how do you develop and find your personal style? My answer may sound glib but it's true:

> If you want to develop a cohesive body of work to develop your visual voice and style, then not only do you have to make a lot of quilts, but you also have to take it seriously, learn to work independently, and learn to embrace the idea of making mistakes and inevitably some really bad art!

Not all the quilts you make will be works of art, and that's good! You'll learn just as much, if not more, from quilts you *don't* like—and quilts that just *don't* work—than you will from quilts you *do* like or that *do* work. But in order to learn from them, you need to understand how to critique your work.

The words *critique* and *criticism* are not interchangeable. A critique should not be a negative experience, whether you're giving one or receiving one. It's a learning experience. It's about evaluating the work, learning from it, and using that information to inform your next piece. Think about keeping a notebook where you can write down notes about the piece you are evaluating so that you can refer back to them later. Doing this can be very helpful when you are building a series of work—it gives you a road map to look back on to see the progression from one piece to the next. Having that documentation to refer back to will keep you from making the same mistakes twice and reminds you why you made the choices that you did with each piece.

Boxed In, 62″ × 35″

CRITIQUING YOUR WORK

When you finish a quilt, leave it for a day or two. Come back to it, hang it up on a neutral background, and make some notes. You might start by evaluating it based on Principles of Design (page 11). Not all of these will relate to every art quilt you make—choose the ones that can be applied to your piece.

Balance Is the composition balanced, or does it feel heavy or lopsided? Does it feel that way because of the colors or the imagery? Is there too much empty space, or is the composition too crowded?

Movement and rhythm Does the finished artwork draw the eye around the work or to an intended area? If the intention was to make the viewer feel movement, does it succeed?

Contrast Do the sizes, colors, values, shapes, and so on have enough contrast to engage the viewer's eye, or does the work look flat, dull, or repetitious?

Proportion Do the elements or imagery in the work relate to each other to create a harmonious whole?

Space Have you used the positive and negative space effectively?

Pattern Is there visual harmony created by the use of the repeating images?

Variety Is there enough variety in the design to keep the viewer engaged and keep their eye moving around the work?

Emphasis If the work has an intended focal point, does it draw the viewer's eye there successfully?

Unity Are the elements, components, and colors harmonious and visually satisfying when viewed as a whole?

In addition to the principles of design, evaluate the work on the basis of:

Craftsmanship Are the materials that were used the appropriate ones? Was the quality of the materials used acceptable? Were the materials easy to manipulate and work with? Did they perform the way you wanted them to?

Techniques Were the appropriate techniques used? Do they enhance or detract from the intended result? Do the techniques used need to be refined before using again?

Mood Has the mood that you're trying to convey with the work been achieved?

Finishing and presentation Does the work hang the way it was intended? Does the binding or finished edge enhance the overall design? Is the way the work is displayed (sleeve and rod, stretcher bars, framed, or some other finishing technique) presenting it in the best way?

Not all of these will relate to every art quilt you make—you'll need to choose the ones that can be applied to the quilt that you're evaluating.

Use the answers from your critique to inform the direction and decisions for your next piece. When each piece is done, critique it and continue repeating this process with each new piece you make. Don't skip the critique step! It gives you an opportunity to consider what you've done and what changes you'd like to make in your next piece before you start it (see Ask: What If …?, below). Even if you're not working in a series, you should always hang up your work, step back from it, and spend some time asking some "What if …?" questions about it. It's a valuable learning experience and opportunity for growth—don't skip it!

Ask: What If …?

Ask yourself these questions when you evaluate your finished quilt:

What if I …

… change the size?

… change the technique?

… combine the technique with another one?

… change the focal point?

… add another shape?

… change the balance?

… move an element?

… add some texture?

… take out some texture?

… change the material used?

… change the value?

… add contrast?

… change the scale?

Writing an Artist Statement

At some point on your artistic journey, you will probably need to write an artist statement, whether it's a detailed statement, perhaps for a specific piece of artwork that you're submitting for consideration for an exhibit, or a general statement, for a website or exhibit catalog, for example. Before you jump in and start writing, it's important to understand what an artist statement is, what purpose it serves, and what guidelines to keep in mind while writing one. Knowing this before you start writing will help make the process easier, and you'll end up with a more effective statement.

WHAT IS AN ARTIST STATEMENT?

An artist statement is a one to three paragraph narrative that gives the reader insightful information about the inspiration, techniques, tools, materials, and processes that you used to create your quilts. It's a valuable tool that can help create a connection between the viewer and your quilts. Think of it as an opportunity to give the viewer some insight into your artistic process and the story or philosophy (if there is one) behind your artwork.

STATEMENT VERSUS BIO

An artist statement is different from a bio. Your artist statement should always be written in the first person rather than the third person style used for a bio. A bio is typically short, two or three sentences, and may include highlights from your resume, such as exhibitions, books, your education, and awards. When you write an article for a magazine they typically ask for a short bio.

My bio is short and just hits the highlights:

> Sue Bleiweiss creates vibrant, colorful art quilts, intended to delight the eye of the viewer and draw them in for a closer look. The author of several books, she has written numerous articles for *Quilting Arts Magazine* and has appeared on *Quilting Arts TV* and *The Quilt Show* with Alex Anderson and Ricky Tims. Sue's award-winning quilts have been exhibited internationally and reside in private collections all over the world.

WRITING YOUR STATEMENT

Writing an artist statement takes time. It's not something you should rush to jot down in a hurry ten minutes before you need it. If you do, your statement will reflect that and you'll have lost your opportunity to connect the reader or the juror with your artwork. You may have to write and edit several drafts of your statement before you have one that you're happy with. Here are four key points to keep in mind before you begin writing:

1. *Keep it simple.*

   Your statement is your opportunity to tell people the how and why about your art. It should not be filled with "artspeak" and fancy words that makes the reader think, *What the heck does that mean?* It should be written as if you were standing next to the person, having a conversation about your artwork. Do not tell the reader what they should see in your art. Remember art is subjective and everyone interprets what they see in it differently. What you see and what the viewer sees may be two very different things.

2. *Tell the reader why you do what you do.*

   Explain (briefly) why you choose to create this kind of art and use the techniques and materials that you do. You might want to include information about your motivation to create a piece of work for a particular subject matter or what or who inspired you to create it.

3. *Tell the reader how you do it.*

   Without going into all the nitty-gritty details, you should include a sentence or two that describes the techniques and materials you've used in your process. Maybe you dyed the fabrics, used paint, screen printing, hand quilted, or used some other techniques to create your quilt. It shouldn't be a step-by-step guide, nor should it include every single technique you used. Keep it to the primary techniques and materials used.

4. *Keep it short.*

   If your statement is too long, you will lose the reader's attention. The purpose of your statement is not to tell the reader about your entire artistic journey. It's not the place to talk about your degrees, hobbies, and all the art techniques you've explored over the years. Your statement shouldn't be long sentences filled with artspeak and complicated words that need explanation. Your statement needs to be clear, well written, and easy to understand.

Getting Started

If you're having trouble getting started on your first draft, begin by writing some individual sentences or words about your work. Don't worry if the sentences don't relate. The idea is to just get some thoughts down on paper to use as a jumping-off point. Approach your first draft as if it were an interview, and ask yourself some questions such as:

• How do I begin a quilt?

• What techniques do I use and why?

• What materials do I use and why?

• What about my process do I want the reader to know?

• What is my inspiration?

• What story am I trying to tell?

• Why did I make this?

• Is there a certain color palette I use? Why?

• What five words would I use to describe my quilt?

• Is there a central image or idea in my quilts?

When you have some answers on paper, go back and read through them and start to put them together to form your first draft. This first draft will no doubt be messy and disorganized, but that's okay because your first draft isn't supposed to be your final draft. You may need to read through it several times over the course of several days before you have a finished statement.

As you go through the editing process ask yourself:

• Did I write consistently in the first person throughout the statement?

• Is the average reader going to be able to understand what I've written?

• Is my statement specific to my work or could it apply to any artist's work?

• Does it read like an instruction manual about how to create my art?

WHAT A STRONG ARTIST STATEMENT LOOKS LIKE

Using my own artwork, processes, and techniques as an example, here's what a weak statement might look like:

> I am an artist who works with fabric and thread. My artwork doesn't reference recognizable form. The results are deconstructed to the extent that meaning is shifted and possible interpretation becomes multifaceted. By applying abstraction, I often create work using creative game tactics, but these are never permissive. Play is a serious matter: During the game, different rules apply than in everyday life, and even everyday objects undergo transubstantiation. My works are characterized by the use of every-day objects in an atmosphere of whimsical mentality in which recognition plays an important role.

The example above uses a lot of artspeak and doesn't give the reader any insight into the processes I use, why I use them, or what I am trying to achieve or communicate with my art.

Here's my actual general artist statement:

Working with my own hand-dyed fabrics, my goal is to create vibrant, colorful, and whimsical fiber art collages that intrigue the eye of the viewer and encourage the viewer to take a closer look.

Each piece begins on the pages of my sketchbook where I make several rough sketches of the imagery that I want to work with. Beginning with a small sketch gives me the freedom to explore combinations of images and colors before cutting into any fabrics. My small sketches are enlarged into full-size cartoons that allow me to adjust the scale of the images, and then the actual construction of the piece in fabric begins.

I work with professional fiber dyes, using a process that uses a minimal amount of water to add color to the cloth I use in my fiber art collages. Dyeing my own fabric allows me to maintain a consistent color palette, and I really enjoy that full-circle feeling of starting with plain white cloth and using it to create something that vibrates with color and delights the eye.

This statement clearly gives the reader some insight into what I do, how I do it, and why, without being a step-by-step guide and without being so long that the reader loses interest in it before they get to the last sentence. I use this as my general "about me" statement on my website and for other instances where a statement is required that is not related to a specific piece of art. If I am submitting a piece of work for consideration for an exhibition, then I tailor the statement to that piece of art, referencing the inspiration, techniques, materials, or motivation specific to that piece of work.

While some artists think that their art speaks for itself and therefore they don't need an artist statement, I think that's really just an excuse to avoid writing one. The truth of the matter is that if you want to provide your viewer (or a juror) a way to connect with your quilt beyond just looking at it, then you need to be able to write about it. When your quilt is on display at an exhibition, quilt show, or gallery, you may not always be able to be there in person to talk about it, so your artist statement has to do that for you.

APPENDIX

Easy Fabric Dyeing

With all the fabric choices available, you might wonder why you might want to dye your own fabrics. The answer is simple—it's easy and fun! Starting with plain white cloth and transforming it into something colorful and visually interesting is exciting. It's a full-circle moment when you put that last stitch on the binding of a quilt made with fabric that you dyed yourself.

My method for dyeing fabric is very easy and tends to produce a fabric with an unevenly colored surface which I prefer because it makes for a more interesting piece of fabric to work with. Of course, every artist has a favorite method for dyeing fabric, and you should experiment to find the one that works best for you.

Hand-dyed fabric

SUPPLIES FOR DYEING

Procion dye   Procion dyes are a cold-water, fiber-reactive dye. Procion dye powders are packaged in jars as small as 2 ounces, which is enough to dye several yards of fabric depending on how dark a result you want to achieve. I buy my Procion dye powders premixed online from Dharma Trading Co. (dharmatrading.com) and PRO Chemical & Dye (prochemicalanddye.net) rather than buying primary colors and mixing them to create secondary colors. Store your unused dye powders in a cool dark place and they'll last for years. (If you don't want to wait for dyes to be shipped and don't need much, you can buy smaller quantities of Jacquard Procion dyes at local art supply stores.)

Fabric dyeing supplies

Respirator/face mask   Procion dye powder particles are extremely fine and must never be inhaled. It's imperative to always wear a respirator or dust mask when working with them.

TIP // Safety First

Procion dye powders pose no airborne health hazard once they are mixed with water. However, when the dyes are in powdered form, you must be very careful not to breathe them in. Wear a respirator or dust mask before you open the dye containers. Do not open the containers in front of a fan, open window, or other people or pets, and close them as soon as you finish measuring out the dye.

Fabric   Use fabric labeled PFD (prepared for dyeing); otherwise, you'll need to prewash it using hot water without any fabric softener to remove any sizing before it can be dyed. When using Procion dyes, you'll need to use plant-based fabrics, such as cotton, linen, silk, and rayon.

Soda ash   Soda ash is the chemical that permanently fixes the dye to the fiber. I buy my soda ash in large 50-pound quantities because I dye fabric on a regular basis, but you can find it available in quantities as small as 1 pound. Store unused soda ash in a clearly labeled container in a cool, dry place and it will last indefinitely.

Plastic zip bags   I use 1- and 2-gallon plastic zip bags to dye my fabric in.

Rubber gloves   Always wear rubber gloves when you are dyeing fabric. I like to use long rubber gloves that cover not only my hands but my arms up to the elbow, and I wear an additional pair of gloves under them just in case the outer pair has a tear or hole that I'm not aware of.

Measuring spoons and cups   Once you use your measuring spoons and cups for dyeing, you must never use them for any food purposes. Use a permanent marker to mark them so you don't risk mixing them up with the ones you use for food preparation.

Coffee filters (optional)   I like to strain my mixed dye through a coffee filter before using it to dye my fabric. This screens out any undissolved dye particles that will cause speckling on the surface of the fabric.

Mixing jar   For mixing the dye with water, a plastic jar with a tight-fitting lid large enough to hold a cup of water and the dye powder works perfectly. Just make sure the lid fits securely enough that it doesn't leak when shaken.

5-gallon bucket   I use a 5-gallon bucket to soak my fabric in soda ash before dyeing it.

Shout Color Catcher   When I wash out my dyed fabric I always throw a Shout Color Catcher dye-trapping sheet in the washer. This keeps any dye from migrating from one fabric to another.

Procion Dye Stains

Procion dye will stain your clothes. I've ruined more jeans and sneakers with spilled or splashed dye than I care to admit, so learn from my mistake. No matter how small a quantity of dye you're working with, make sure you're wearing clothing (and footwear!) that you don't mind getting dye on.

It will also stain wood surfaces, tile grout, and so on, so make sure you cover your work surfaces with plastic sheeting in case of drips and spills. I cover the plastic sheeting with old towels which absorb any spills and make clean up easier.

FIVE-STEP FABRIC-DYEING PROCESS

Step 1: Soak the fabric in a solution of soda ash and water.

Fill a large bucket with several gallons of warm water, put on your face mask or respirator, and add at least ½ cup of soda ash for each gallon of water. Warm water helps to dissolve the soda ash more quickly, and you'll be able to tell when the soda ash has completely dissolved because the water in the bucket will look clear. Use an old mixing spoon (that you've marked for dyeing only) to stir the soda ash around in the water to help it dissolve. Cut or tear your fabric into manageable-size pieces (I like to use half-yard pieces.) that will fit comfortably in your zip bags, and add the fabric to the bucket. Soak the fabric in the soda ash/water solution for at least 20 minutes before you dye it.

Dyed fabric swatch cards

Step 2: Mix the dye.

When I mix my dye I use a ratio of 1 teaspoon of dye to 1 cup of water. This results in a rich vibrant color. If you do not want your colors so saturated, you'll need to adjust your measurements based on the results that you want. If you want a lighter result, start with a ¼ or ½ teaspoon of dye. I recommend keeping notes and making samples so that when you find the formula that gives you the result you want, you'll be able to duplicate when you need more. Whenever I dye a piece of fabric using a new color of dye, I write the dye color on a piece of Tyvek with a permanent marker and I safety-pin it to the fabric. This makes it easy to identify the fabric when it comes out of the dryer with all the other fabrics. Once

I've pressed the fabric, I cut off a small swatch and staple it to a card with notes about how much dye, water, and fabric I used to achieve that result.

To mix the dye, put approximately ¼–½ cup of warm water in a jar with a tight-fitting lid and add 1 teaspoon of dye powder. Screw the lid on tightly and shake it really well to dissolve the dye powder.

TIP // Dyeing Black Fabric

I make an exception to my dye formula when I am dyeing black fabric. To get a nice rich black fabric, I use 2 tablespoons of dye to 1 cup of water and I dye the fabric twice. Once the fabric comes out of the washing machine the first time, I mix another dye bath and dye it again.

Step 3: Strain the dye.

This step is optional so you can skip it if you want, but I like to strain my dye because it avoids the problem of any undissolved dye particles coming in contact with the fabric and causing speckling on the surface. I strain the mixed dye through a coffee filter into a measuring cup and add enough water to bring the mixture to 1 cup.

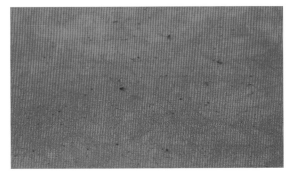

The surface speckles are a result of undissolved dye particles in the dye bath.

Strain the dye through a coffee filter.

Step 4: Dye the fabric.

Remove a piece of the fabric that has been soaking in the soda ash solution for at least 20 minutes and squeeze out the excess water. Add the fabric to a plastic zip bag, pour in the strained dye, and knead the bag to distribute the dye. Now there's nothing to do but wait and let the dye do its job. You may want to knead the bag occasionally to distribute the dye throughout the cloth as it sits in the bag. The less you knead the bag, the more unevenly dyed the surface of your fabric will be. When I dye larger pieces of fabric, I like to open the bag occasionally, reach in, and move the fabric around to make sure that the dye gets into all the nooks and crannies of the crumpled fabric.

Let the fabric soak in the dye.

You should leave your fabric to sit in the dye for at least 4 hours. It's fine to let it soak longer, and I have even let my fabric soak in the dye overnight.

Appendix

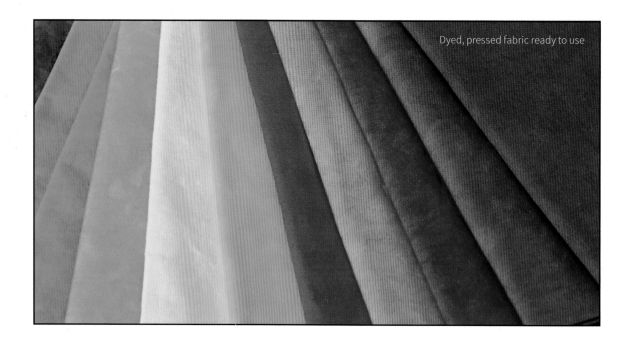

Dyed, pressed fabric ready to use

Step 5: Washing out excess dye.

After the fabrics have soaked in the dye for at least 4 hours, take them out of the bags and squeeze out any excess liquid. Put the fabrics with *like colors together* (meaning, don't put the blues and greens in with the pinks and yellows!) into the washer along with a Shout Color Catcher sheet, and wash them in cold water with regular detergent and with the machine set for at least 2 rinses. Then toss them in the dryer to dry them. When they're out of the dryer, press them with a hot iron and they're ready to use. If you are using your hand-dyed fabrics in a project that will be washed, then you should test to make sure that all the excess dye has been washed out. You can do this by ironing wet fabric between 2 pieces of white fabric or putting the fabric in the sink filled with water to see if the water remains clear. If not, then repeat the wash cycle until you're confident that all the excess dye has been washed out.

TIP // Rinsing the Fabric

When I take the fabrics out of the bag, I don't bother to rinse them under running water until the water runs clear because I'd be at the sink forever. I just squeeze out the excess dye water and then put them in the washer.

...THOR

...g full-
...owing the
...e sidelines for
...ody of work
...d bright
...nade her
first modern quilt in 2016 and was rewarded
with a first-place ribbon for it in the appliqué
category at QuiltCon that same year.

The author of *The Sketchbook Challenge*
and *Colorful Fabric Collage*, she has written
numerous articles for many internationally
published quilting magazines. Her television
appearances include *Quilting Arts TV* and
The Quilt Show with Alex Anderson and
Ricky Tims.

Widely recognized for her signature style of
quilting and design, she loves to teach both in
person and online and share her experiences
and knowledge with other quilters. She
lives in a beautiful little New England town
in Massachusetts where she spends her
weekends hiking or canoeing along the
Nashua River with her husband, Scott.

Visit Sue online!
suebleiweiss.com

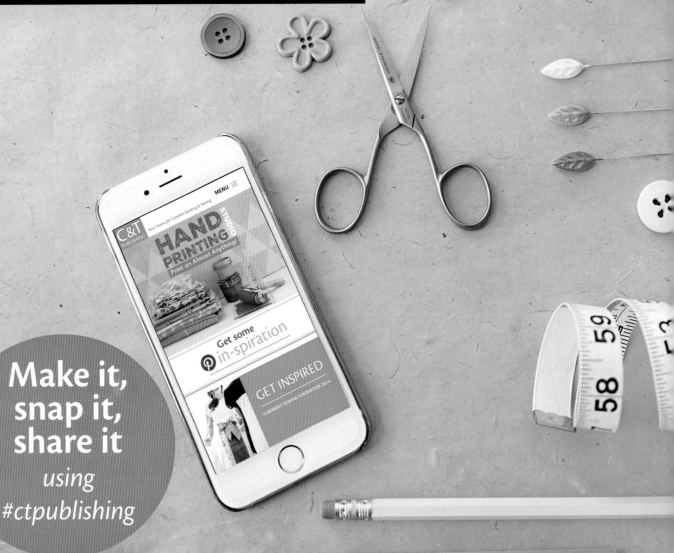

Want even
more creative
content?

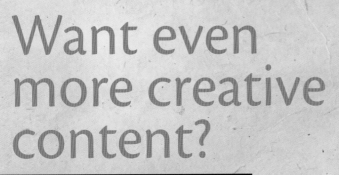

**Make it,
snap it,
share it**
*using
#ctpublishing*